Creative Metal Clay Jewelry

CeCe Wire. *Circle, Circle, Square Pin,* 2001.
1¼ x 1¼ x ¼ in. (3.2 x 3.2 cm x 6 mm).
Silver metal clay, sterling silver, liver-of-
sulfur patina, and steel nuts and bolts.

Creative Metal Clay Jewelry

TECHNIQUES, PROJECTS, INSPIRATION

CeCe Wire

A Division of Sterling Publishing Co., Inc.
New York

DEDICATION

To my friends Cole Michael O'Donnell and
McKenna Leigh O'Donnell

Editor: Suzanne J. E. Tourtillott
Art Director: Celia Naranjo
Photographer: Sandra Stambaugh
Cover Designer: Barbara Zaretsky
Illustrator: Olivier Rollin
Assistant Editor: Veronika Gunter
Art Assistance: Shannon Yokeley
Art Intern: Lorelei Buckley
Editorial Assistance: Delores Gosnell

Library of Congress Cataloging-in-Publication Data

Wire, CeCe.
   Creative metal clay jewelry : techniques, projects, inspiration / by CeCe Wire.—1st ed.
       p. cm.
   Includes index.
   ISBN 1-57990-301-0 (hard)
   1. Jewelry making. 2. Precious metal clay. I. Title.

TT212 .W57 2003
745.594'2—dc21

2002034398

10 9 8 7 6 5 4 3 2

Published by Lark Books, a division of
Sterling Publishing Co., Inc.
387 Park Avenue South, New York, N.Y. 10016

Distributed in Canada by Sterling Publishing,
c/o Canadian Manda Group, One Atlantic Ave., Suite 105
Toronto, Ontario, Canada M6K 3E7

Distributed in the U.K. by Guild of Master Craftsman Publications Ltd., Castle Place, 166 High Street,
Lewes, East Sussex, England, BN7 1XU

Tel: (+ 44) 1273 477374, Fax: (+ 44) 1273 478606,
Email: pubs@thegmcgroup.com, Web: www.gmcpublications.com

Distributed in Australia by Capricorn Link (Australia) Pty Ltd.,
P.O. Box 704, Windsor, NSW 2756 Australia

If you have questions or comments about this book, please contact:

Lark Books
67 Broadway
Asheville, NC 28801
(828) 236-9730

Manufactured InChina

1-577990-301-0

A Note About Suppliers

Usually, the supplies you need for making the projects in Lark books can be found at your local craft supply store, discount mart, home improvement center, or retail shop relevant to the topic of the book. Occasionally, however, you may need to buy materials or tools from specialty suppliers. In order to provide you with the most up-to-date information, we have created suppliers listings on our Web site, which we update on a regular basis. Visit us at www.larkbooks.com, click on "Craft Supply Sources," and then click on the relevant topic. You will find numerous companies listed with their web address and/or mailing address and phone number.

Contents

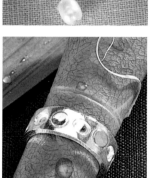

How Metal Clay Changed My Life

TOP: CeCe Wire. *Circle, Circle, Square Pin,* 2001. 1¼ x 1¼ x ¼ in. (3.2 x 3.2 cm x 6 mm). Silver metal clay, sterling silver, liver-of-sulfur patina, and steel nuts and bolts. PHOTO BY CRAIG DEMARTINO.

BOTTOM: CeCe Wire. *Bead #3,* 1998. 1⅞ x ⅜ x ⅜ in. (4.7 cm x 9.5 x 9.5 mm). Silver metal clay and sterling silver ball chain. PHOTO BY CRAIG DEMARTINO.

I WAS FIRST INTRODUCED TO METAL CLAY when I read a 1995 magazine article by artist Tim McCreight. It was about a new material, developed in Japan, that looks and feels like clay and yet, by firing it, it becomes pure, solid metal. At first I thought I misunderstood. I thought, "A clay that turns into silver defies all reason; there must be some mistake." As a jeweler, metal clay seemed to offer so many possibilities I couldn't sleep that night. I worked until the wee hours of the morning trying to capture in my sketchbook the hundreds of ideas that swam through my mind. I could make hollow silver beads, sculpted forms, work with enamel, carve dry clay on a lathe, and bypass traditional lost-wax casting with an easier and faster method. I was amazed.

I'm pretty sure I was one of the very first people in the United States to purchase and use metal clay. Two weeks after learning where I might purchase it, I had sculpted, fired, and enameled a piece—and then displayed it in a group exhibition. I was on a path that forever changed the way I worked as a metalsmith, a path that changed my life.

The story doesn't end there. A short time later, I was teaching jewelry at a community college and I brought my first pieces to class with me one night. My students were curious to learn more about the stuff that I was so excited about. Those early learning sessions, though energizing to all of us, helped me realize that I wanted to get some professional training, and that doing so would give me the confidence and knowledge to further spread the metal clay gospel. I took Tim's class and eventually gained enough experience to teach other teachers about metal clay. I'm now the director of the largest metal clay guild in the world—and that is how metal clay changed my life.

 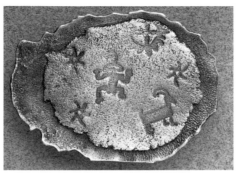

I hope that working with this material will change your life as
well, perhaps not in as dramatic a way as it did mine, but maybe it
will change the way you relax at night, how you make meaningful
gifts for the special people in your life, or help you add new techniques to the art forms that you're already skilled at. Lampworked
and fused dichroic glass, enamel, and beads all gain new life when
they're incorporated into metal clay creations. Metal clay lets you
design every aspect of a piece, with all the components made by
your own hand. You'll soon realize you've discovered a whole new
creative world in amazing metal clay.

Discovering Metal Clay

METAL CLAY IS AN AMAZING ART MATERIAL made of three ingredients: water, an organic binder, and pure metal particles of either silver or gold. The particles of binder and metal are so fine that they resemble cornstarch. In its unfired form, metal clay is soft; you can manipulate it just like other clays. Roll it out or model it, pierce, cut, or tear it, join or assemble separate pieces of it, then texture and fire it!

The magic happens in the firing process, once the metal clay becomes pure silver or gold. My friend Jean Campbell, the editor of *Beadwork* magazine, has referred to this transformation as "kiln alchemy." And although the process of turning a claylike material into silver or gold sounds like alchemy, the transformation is not so mysterious once you understand the process by which it changes from a soft, pliable material to a solid precious metal. (Yes, it really is a precious metal!) It can be buffed, burnished, polished, soldered, hammered, formed, enameled, or patinated. Virtually anything you can create with traditional fine silver or pure gold, you can make with metal clay. Also, air spaces trapped in the firing process create a material that is more porous and less dense than conventional sheet silver or sheet gold. This is a great advantage for making jewelry because you are free to design large pieces with less weight.

There are three formulas of metal clay. Each one is fired for a specific length of time (here referred to as quick-, medium-, and slow-fire), and each is available in lump form. The medium-fire version is also available in several other forms, such as paste. Choose the formula and form best suited to your design needs and working method.

Lump metal clay is the most versatile of the forms. It has the look and feel of a fine porcelain clay body: ultrasmooth and highly refined. Don't be misled by the word clay, though; there really isn't any clay in metal clay, just water, organic binder, and precious metal particles. Once the piece is completely dry only organic binder and precious metal particles remain, and you can fire it in a small electric kiln; the newer formulas may be fired with a butane torch, but a

CeCe Wire. *Blazer Pin,* 2001. 1¼ x ¾ x ¼ in. (3.2 x 1.9 cm x 6 mm). Silver metal clay, sterling silver, enamel, and liver-of-sulfur patina. Private collection of Dik Munson. PHOTO BY CRAIG DEMARTINO

kitchen oven or toaster oven won't get hot enough. By the way, even though metal clay is certified nontoxic, be sure to use common-sense precautions when handling it.

As the piece is heated, the organic binder burns away and only the precious metal particles remain. In this early stage of firing, the piece is fragile; it's not yet a solid metal because the metal particles haven't yet bonded together. (If the kiln is bumped during this stage the piece could fall apart!) When your design reaches the required temperature, the metal particles start to fuse together—the technical term is *sinter*—and the result is a beautiful silver or gold construction.

Finally, as you begin to discover the very different qualities of pre- and post-fired metal clay, you'll find it helpful to be familiar with some terms from other art media; see the sidebar, The Dual Nature of Metal Clay.

Each formula has its own special characteristics, so let's take some time to learn more about the evolution of this fascinating and versatile metal product.

First Generation: Slow-Fire Silver & Gold Metal Clays

The original formula of silver and gold metal clays has metal particles that average about 20 microns in size. Their shape is fluffy and irregular (imagine a cotton ball), and during firing they shrink at a rate of 28 percent, resulting in a light and porous metal. The two-hour firing time is the longest of all three formulas, but the clay has some special qualities, too. I suggest using this formula—which is only made in lump form—for modeling, carving, or if the main focus of the design is on texture. Its consistency is perfect for the kind of moist sculpting techniques used for the African Mask pin on page 115. You'll discover that it's also great for pressing textures into the moist clay and for capturing details for intricate designs, which become even more detailed after firing, since they shrink proportionally along with the piece itself.

This earliest formula for metal clay has a higher ratio of water and binder, so it dries slowly with less cracking, and is easier for a beginner to work with. I don't recommend it for pieces that will get

The Dual Nature of Metal Clay

The working quality of metal clay changes as you work with it, so we use descriptive terms from two very different media—both clay and metal—to help describe this changeable substance.

To design and build a form from clay, ceramists model and join basic units such as slabs, coils, or balls. They do their work in a world defined by water, or the lack of it. They say leather hard to describe clay in which most of the moisture has been driven off: firm, yet with a flexible, workable quality, like leather. Bone dry clay is like a desert floor; arid, warm, and brittle. It's ready to be transformed by fire.

As you move to the firing stage and beyond, you enter the realm of the jeweler. Silver and gold are durable metals, still malleable, but essentially rigid and resistant. Surface is everything. A jeweler's finishes describe metal clay's light-reflective qualities. A mirror finish is bright, polished, and perfect; satin or matte finishes are soft, like an overcast day.

So, is metal clay more like clay or metal? You decide.

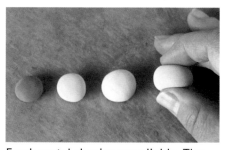

Fresh metal clay is very pliable. The dark ball is gold; the others are silver.

The Mark of Metal Quality

If you sell your work, you'll want to be sure to hallmark it. A hallmark is a stamp made in the precious metal that guarantees its quality. Mark the silver "999" or "FS" (called fine silver by jewelers), and the gold "24k." Inscribe this on the back side with a pin tool, while the clay is moist or dry, along with your name or a logo and the year the piece was completed. Or, wait until after the piece is fired and stamp your work with a steel quality-marking stamp, available from a jeweler's supply source.

a lot of wear, though, because even after proper firing this porous version could break later under the stress of normal wear. And if you want to use 925 sterling silver or 950 silver findings, such as pin backs or jump rings, you'll have to attach them after firing—these alloys melt if they're fired with the clay itself.

Like original-formula silver metal clay, gold metal clay has the same particle size and shape and shrinkage rate, though it fires at a slightly higher temperature. Because gold is costly, you might want to start by creating designs that use touches of gold on mostly silver pieces. You must fire a gold-and-silver piece only to the silver firing temperature; firing it to the higher gold temperature melts the silver! This slightly underfired gold won't be as brilliant or as strong as a higher-fired gold (you'll find a solution to this dilemma in the Firing section on page 41). Before firing, gold metal clay is an odd yellow ocher color; after the transformation, it's the most amazingly beautiful gold I've ever seen. However, because pure gold metal clay is soft, it isn't suitable for clasps or other objects that need strength; pure gold is too easily misshapen.

Second Generation: Medium-Fire Silver Metal Clay

Medium-fire silver metal clay is ideal for wearable pieces and parts like rings and clasps because it's stronger and denser than the original (slow-fire) silver or gold metal clay. Perhaps the biggest breakthrough of this second generation is that this newer formula comes in several exciting new forms: lump, paste, syringe, and paper, for even more creative possibilities than ever. It's also possible to use it in combination with fine jewelry materials, such as enamel (see the Avocado Salt Cellar on page 133) or fused glass (turn to page 92 to see the Moon in the Sky pendant). This is because these materials liquify during firing and they're less likely to interact at points of contact with the denser medium-fire metal. It won't work as well as slow-fire clay, though, for techniques such as carving because it tends to crumble when it's cut at the bone-dry stage. You can use medium-fire clay in combination with any other formula of metal clay, though you may need to fire the individual elements separately and join them together later.

CeCe Wire. *Square Pin,* 2000.
1½ x 1½ x ⅜ in. (3.8 x 3.8 cm x 9.5 mm).
Silver metal clay, sterling silver,
and liver-of-sulfur patina.
PHOTO BY CRAIG DEMARTINO.

At present, two different manufacturers make silver metal clay with shorter firing times than the original formula. Their composition is similar to one another and they're handled in the same basic way. The silver particles are smaller—only 5 microns in size—and they're shaped like spheres, resulting in a denser fired metal than the first-generation clay. Because this formula has less water and binder, it dries quickly and cracks more easily, making it a little more challenging to work with. A big plus, though, is that it shrinks less—10 to 15 percent.

Best of all, the basic firing time is just 10 minutes, yet you have the option to fire this newer material at lower temperatures for longer periods, too. This is a distinct advantage if you're making jewelry pieces because at this lower temperature you'll be able to include 925 sterling silver or 950 silver jewelry findings, such as pin backs and jump rings, during the firing of the metal clay piece itself. These findings would melt at higher temperatures. In such cases, be sure to refer to the firing chart on page 40 for detailed information about how to extend the firing time so you can lower the temperature.

CeCe Wire. *Asian Assemblage,* 2001. 2¼ x 2¼ x ¼ in (5.7 x 5.7 cm x 6 mm). PMC+, woven PMC+ paper, sterling silver, brass, Nepalese chain, antique Chinese coin, carved horn, ostrich egg shell. PHOTO BY SANDRA STAMBAUGH.

A WEALTH OF METAL CLAY FORMS

When paste, paper, and syringe forms of medium-fire metal clay became available, the range of creative possibilities really opened up. Even though the lump form can be shaped almost any way you like, these other forms make some modeling and repair techniques quick and simple to do. Depending on which form you use, the metal clay varies somewhat in particle size and shape, type of binder, and the proportions of the various ingredients, but the three elements (water, organic binder, and silver particles) remain the same.

Paste

Metal clay paste is a factory-made, wet mix of clay and water. It's not only useful straight from the jar for repairing cracks or breaks, if you let some of the moisture evaporate you can use it to join metal clay to itself—either moist, leather hard, or bone dry. You can even use it to attach two fired pieces together.

Paste form of metal clay

Paste also may be used to create a texture. It can be applied with a pallet knife to leather-hard or bone-dry clay much the same way you'd spackle a plaster wall. This technique was used for the Stormy Wave bead on page 129, and it's a practical way to use up your slip if you've accumulated too much of it.

One great way to get a realistic, detailed "cast" of an organic object is to paint on several layers of thinned paste. The Twig & Leaf Condiment Spoon on page 137 is an example of this amazing technique.

Syringe

This is really versatile stuff! A ceramic or polymer clay artist would recognize the syringe container as similar to that of an *extruder*, a kind of caulking gun. The plunger extrudes a narrow clay coil through the syringe tip. Use this form to repair pieces made from any form of silver metal clay, as a surface decoration, or to make a bezel to hold a stone like the ones in the Under the Elm pin on page 120. Although it's the same basic formula as the paste, the syringe clay has more binder and less water, and its thicker consistency holds its shape well. You might fill your own empty syringe with slip made from the lump form of metal clay, to which has been added a very small drop of water-soluble gel glue. You'll need to experiment to get the right consistency—something between heavy cream and toothpaste.

Here's a little secret I learned from Mary Ann Devos, director of education for the PMCConnection. To keep the syringe juicy and ready to go between uses, put the open end of the syringe in a cut-flower vial filled with distilled water. Otherwise, you'll have to add the dry plug of clay from the tip to your slip container.

Paper

Paper metal clay, you say? Wow, what a great idea! Of course it's perfect for the Japanese art of origami, but I've fallen in love with it because I can punch, braid, or weave it for a delicious variety of pat-

Syringe and paper forms of
metal clay

terns. Use craft punches or decorative scissors to get crisp details or cut it into threadlike strips and weave with it. These techniques are simply not possible with the lump form of metal clay.

Metal clay paper feels like a thin sheet of rubber but remains flexible and pliable until it's fired, and it has the unique property of never drying out. Store the metal clay paper in the sealed package or in a resealable plastic food storage bag to keep the silver particles from *oxidizing* and turning brown. The thickness of these fired sheets is 26 gauge, or .018 inch, too thin to be practical for jewelry unless you join it to a backing layer of rolled-out lump clay; the Simple Weave earrings on page 61 use this technique.

Next Generation: Quick-Fire Silver Metal Clay

Because of its lower firing temperature and 60-second firing time, this denser, stronger material is even better suited to use with other media. The lower firing temperature makes it less likely that certain materials, such as glass, will interact with the clay as it's converted to silver.

The quick-fire silver particles are an assortment of shapes and sizes, with only enough water and binder to hold them together in the clay form. This makes for a stiffer, drier, and slightly more challenging material to work with. Like the medium-fire formula, the quick-fire clay shrinks 12 to 15 percent. You can even bypass the need for a kiln, instead using a butane torch (like the ones used to carmelize sugar on crème brûlée). Another plus is that it's the strongest formula of silver clay yet made, so you can use if for pieces like rings, clasps, or cuff-style bracelets that will take a lot of wear. Though presently available only in lump form, you'll soon see it in the versatile paste, syringe, and paper forms, too.

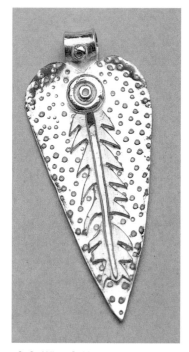

CeCe Wire. *Golden Vein,* 2000.
3 x 1¼ x ¼ in (7.6 x 3.2 cm x 6 mm).
Silver and gold metal clays.
PHOTO BY SANDRA STAMBAUGH.

Tools, Equipment & Space

AS WITH ANY CRAFT MEDIUM, you'll need to make an initial investment in the tools, equipment, and work space. Here, I'll introduce you to the basic set of tools I rely on whenever I make a design in metal clay. Next are my recommendations for items that I use for many of the projects in this book, followed by some great stuff that I think makes creativity really spark. Finally, we'll look at the ideal work space, plus what you need to know about firing equipment.

The Basic Toolbox

This basic collection of tools is essential for nearly every project. Keep them organized at your work space so you'll be ready to create metal clay pieces whenever inspiration strikes.

Clockwise from upper left: Heavyweight plastic food wrap, slip containers, olive oil, hand balm, PVC pipe rolling pin, playing cards, mat-board spacers, watercolor paintbrush, water dish, spray mister, work surface

Rolling Pin

The most economical way to use the lump form of metal clay is to roll it out to a flat sheet, much like rolling out pie dough. For this you'll need some type of plastic rolling pin. I use a piece of PVC pipe (available at home improvement centers), ¾ inch (1.9 cm) in diameter and 9 inches (22.9 cm) long. You can cut this material easily with a hacksaw or chop saw, either to the length of both your hands or so it fits conveniently in your toolbox. Don't use a wooden rolling pin; the metal clay particles are so fine they'll stick to its porous surface.

Spacers

Use spacers to roll out lump clay to the desired and consistent thickness. I like to roll out the original-formula metal clay to the thickness of mat board, or ¹⁄₁₆ inch (1.6 mm), so I keep two 1 x 8-inch (2.5 x 20.3 cm) strips of it at my work bench for this purpose. I also keep a dozen or so playing cards handy, because I can easily stack them on top of each other—three, four, five, or six layers deep—for a variety of thickness choices. For medium-fire metal clay I use three playing cards. Anything thinner might develop holes during firing, and very thin objects aren't practical for use or wear.

Work Surfaces

You'll need both flexible and rigid work surfaces. I use a ¼-inch-thick (6 mm) sheet of plate glass, cut to 18 x 24 inches (45.7 x 61 cm), for the rigid one, as well as several sizes of flexible nonstick baking sheet. Your local glass supplier can cut the plate glass, then sand and finish the edges so it's safe to handle. Find the baking sheet at a gourmet cooking store and cut it with scissors to any size you like. When I travel or teach classes, I take an 8½ x 11-inch (21.6 x 27.9 cm) piece of either styrene plastic sheet or mat board, plus a flexible clear plastic report cover.

Slip Container

You'll need a small airtight container, such as an empty 35-millimeter film container, for slip. Remember, you're working with a precious metal and will want to save and use every particle of it. Due

Chris Darway. *Necklace,* 1998.
16-inch (40.6 cm) length.
Pendant: 1½ x 3 x ¼ in. (3.8 x 7.6 cm x 6 mm).
Silver metal clay; titanium, 14k gold.
PHOTO BY CHET BOLINS. Private collection.

to the differences between the formulas, keep one container for original formula silver metal clay, another for the medium- and quick-fire silver metal clays, and a third one if you work with gold metal clay.

Moisture Maintainers

It's important to keep the metal clay moist while you're working. Keep some fine olive oil or hand balm with olive oil, a round #2 paintbrush and clean small bowl, a fine-mist spray bottle, and some heavyweight plastic wrap for food all close by.

Drying Tools

Before firing it, air-dry metal clay—or for quicker results, apply gentle heat to it. The tools are inexpensive and easy to find.

Drying Rack. If you're going to create several pieces it's more efficient to group them together according to their similar firing times, and color-coded drying racks make that easier to do. I suggest that you make a separate drying rack in a different color for each formula, using colorful plastic needlepoint canvas and craft sticks. For the frame, glue together the craft sticks with wood glue, then cut the plastic canvas to fit it.

Hair Dryer. If you're anxious to fire your design right away, use a hair dryer to speed the drying process. However, be advised that using a hair dryer may cause cracks to form on the surface of the metal clay. If this happens, use slip to fill them in, as described in the Repairs sections on pages 34 and 36.

Warming Plate. My preferred method for drying pieces is to place my work on a coffee cup–warming plate. It's compact and portable, and dries the piece with gentle, even heat. Please remember to use tweezers to remove the piece, and allow the piece to cool before touching it.

Wire Brush

After firing your design, the first finishing step is to use a brass wire brush, available at hardware stores. These are usually 7 inches (17.8 cm) long, with several rows of brass wire bristles. Don't use

Left to right: hair dryer, drying rack, warming plate

brushes made with steel wire! The steel will turn the silver clay gray, and your piece will look like it's made of pewter, not fine silver. Steel brushes also discolor gold metal clay. There's more information on a variety of final-finish tools and supplies on pages 43–45.

Beyond the Basic Toolbox

These handy items are used for many, but not all, of the projects in this book. Many of them are available either through craft, art, jewelry, polymer clay, ceramic clay, or metal clay suppliers.

Cutting Tools

You have several choices for cutting metal clay. I use a craft knife for most of my cutting, but for long, straight cuts it's easier to use a tissue blade. If you use a drawing template to get a specific shape, a pin or needle tool (available from clay and metal clay suppliers) is the right choice for cutting it out. Even though it creates a ragged edge, it can be filed off later. Collect an assortment of beverage stirrers and straws of different diameters for cutting holes to hang cord, chain, or earring wires.

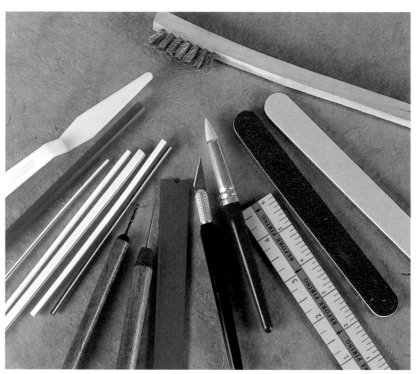

Left to right: plastic palette knife, hole cutters, hand drill, pin tool, tissue blade, craft knife, blender tool, shrinkage ruler, emery boards, wire brush.

Blender Tool

When joining seams, a blender tool is just the thing to make them disappear. In traditional art practice, these tools are used to blend oil pastels and other soft media. A good all-purpose size is a #6 blender tool. I use a brand that color-codes the tips according to their degree of flexibility.

Ins & Outs of Shrinkage

There are times when you'll want to know how much smaller the size of your piece will be after firing. The most reliable way to calculate this change is to use the shrinkage ruler to measure an actual-size preliminary sketch or template shape. Find your original measurement on the ruler; the finished size appears opposite it. Remember that slow-fire clay shrinks 28 percent, while quick- and medium-fire clays shrink from 10 to 15 percent.

If you don't have a ruler, use the enlarge/reduce function on a photocopier. Enlarge the drawing or template shape to 128 percent for slow-fire metal clay or 112 percent for medium- or quick-fire clay, then create the piece at the enlarged size.

Silver metal clay amulet:
1 x ¼ x ¼ in. (2.5 cm x 6 x 6 mm).
Polymer clay amulet: 1¼ x ⅜ x ⅜
in. (3.2 cm x 9.5 x 9.5 mm).

Plastic Pallet Knife

You'll need a plastic pallet knife to make—and sometimes apply—slip. Don't use a metal pallet knife with metal clay; certain metals react with the binder.

Shrinkage Tools

In some cases, you may want to know how the clay's shrinkage will affect the final size of your design. Use the shrinkage ruler, available from metal clay suppliers, if math wasn't your best subject in school, or use a photocopier. Read the Ins & Outs of Shrinkage sidebar, at left, for a quick lesson on the subject.

Emery Boards

File smooth any rough edges of bone-dry metal clay using a series of emery boards. Start with the coarse grit, then finish with a fine emery board.

Linoleum Carving Tool

Use a linoleum-carving tool to cut into the surface of bone-dry clay. Designed for linoleum block printing, you'll find it in the printmaking section of an art supply store. The basic tool holds any one of a variety of different-shaped cutting tips that create different looks. I recommend that you start with a #1.

Drill

Although most times you'll make holes in the clay while it's still moist, you also have the option of drilling the fired metal clay with a metal (not wood) drill bit and a motorized flexible-shaft tool (or drill press or hand drill) instead. As with all motorized tools, wear eye protection and follow the manufacturer's safety instructions. Yet another solution for making holes in the metal is to use a hand drill with a metal bit and good old-fashioned muscle power. You may need to file down the burrs with a jeweler's needle file.

Burnisher

A glossy, smooth, high-polish finish on silver or gold is easy to get with a burnishing tool. These are available in the printmaking section of art supply stores or from jewelry suppliers. Choose from several different styles, in various lengths, with curved or straight points. Try more than one type to find the burnisher you like best.

Needle File

Normally you'll refine the edges of your metal clay piece with an emery board before firing it, but if you forget, smooth the edges of the fired metal later with a jeweler's needle file. Select a fine- or medium-cut file.

Polishing Cloth

This jeweler's cloth is impregnated with a special compound that keeps the metal's surface clean and free of tarnish.

Spatula

A stainless steel double-ended spatula is great for picking up metal clay from a rigid work surface.

Creativity Tools

Lots of great tools available from ceramic clay suppliers make working with all types of clay easier. It's certainly possible to make wonderful metal clay pieces without these tools, but they're nice additions to your basic metal

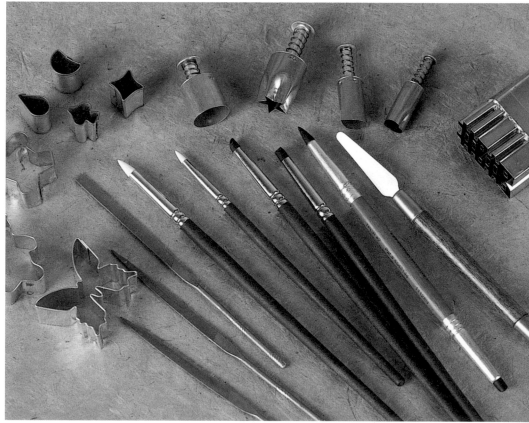

Clockwise from left: cookie, canapé, and pattern cutters; spatula; a selection of blender tools; jeweler's needle files

Pattern cutters and decorative scissors work well with the paper form of metal clay.

clay toolbox. If you can afford to acquire them, they'll speed your creative process. Look through suppliers' catalogs for even more inspiration. Another source for tools is polymer clay suppliers. Polymer clay artists have borrowed the smaller ceramic tools and have even scaled down many of their larger tools, so they are appropriate for jewelry-size projects.

Cutters

In your kitchen you'll find an assortment of tools that make crisp, repeatable shapes easy and fast. Perhaps you have cookie or canapé cutters collecting dust in a drawer. These are great for cutting out crisp shapes like the Teddy Bear pin on page 109. If you don't own them already, shop for a wide assortment of shapes and sizes at gourmet cooking stores. Once you've used them with clay, though, don't use them for food anymore.

Use decorative craft scissors to cut paper metal clay, or buy a set of brass pattern cutters with spring-loaded plungers for rolled-out lump clay. The plunger makes removing bits of cut clay as easy as the push of a button. You'll find circles, stars, squares, diamonds, flowers, leaves, and heart shapes, in a variety of sizes and mixed-pattern sets. I used the flower and circle cutters to make the Groovy Flowers earrings on page 52.

Note: Don't let galvanized metals, tin, aluminum, aluminum foil, cast iron, or anything that rusts or is of unknown composition come into contact with metal clay. These metals react with the binder and can create irreversible contamination. Stainless steel, copper, brass, plastics, and glass don't cause any problems.

Plastic Texture Sheets

It's amazing what a wide vocabulary of textures you'll have at hand with plastic texture sheets. They were designed with the train hobbyist in mind, and they're available through polymer clay suppliers and hobby shops. They make pressing texture into metal clay a source of instant gratification. You'll have a wide vocabulary to choose from because they come in a variety of patterns such as bricks, leaves, and stones.

Plastic Drawing Templates

An assortment of plastic drawing templates can be found at art or drafting supply stores. I like to have a wide selection of drawing templates, different shapes and sizes, to pick from. These also are useful in the design stage, when they can help you to determine the final size of any fired template shape. For more information, see the sidebar on shrinkage on page 18.

More Blenders

Expand your collection of blender tools by trying those with different shaped tips: conical, chisel point, and beveled. Some makers color-code the tips according to their degree of flexibility. Try the softest tip first, until you get the feel for the tool.

Kilns & Torches

The formula you've used to make a metal-clay design will help you decide whether to use a kiln or a torch for firing. Be sure to read about how to choose the best firing method, on page 39, before making your purchase. Both firing methods will require some additional accessory equipment, which may be found at a jewelry or metal clay supply house.

THE KILN: RELIABLE, EVEN HEAT

Original-formula metal clay must be fired for two hours in a kiln. Although the two newer formulas offer you the option of using a high-temperature torch and much shorter firing times, I recommend you use a kiln for all your firing. You'll need a small electric kiln with a programmable pyrometer (a device which monitors the kiln's internal temperature); these are available through metal clay suppliers. Because they're designed specially for metal clay, these kilns carefully maintain even heat through the sintering phase, then automatically maintain a preset firing, or holding, temperature. They also can be used for small-scale glass slumping, glass annealing, and traditional enameling. Unfortunately, the temperature in a ceramic kiln fluctuates too much, and heats too unevenly, to fire metal clay without the risk of melting some pieces.

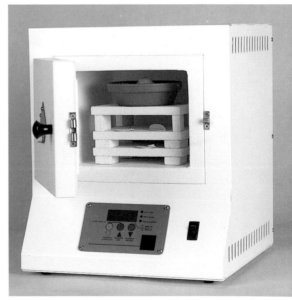

Programmable electric kiln designed to fire metal clay

Left to right: vermiculite and alumina hydrate support materials in terra-cotta saucer.

You'll want to furnish your little boxy kiln "room" with—what else?—kiln furniture. Fire flat pieces on an unglazed ceramic tile, a soldering pad, or on a kiln shelf. To fire many pieces at one time, stack shelves on kiln blocks. The blocks shown in the photo on page 21 measure 1 x 2 x ¼ inches (2.5 x 5.1 cm x 6 mm) to allow for several different stacking height options, and they're made from a soldering pad. Metal clay suppliers carry a shelf kit with three shelves and 12 kiln blocks.

To withstand the high heat of the kiln, three-dimensional objects, like beads, must sit in a granular support material during firing. Choose one of two reusable materials: either alumina hydrate (available from clay suppliers) or vermiculite (find it in any gardening department).

Vermiculite is made from mica, which darkens after the first firing. After several firings, it begins to break down into smaller and smaller pieces, so replace it occasionally. Alumina hydrate, though more expensive than vermiculite, lasts forever—or at least for a very long time. Fill a terra-cotta saucer with either of these materials, and set the piece halfway into it, as shown. Wear a respirator to avoid breathing the dust of alumina hydrate; long-term exposure to it is dangerous. Wash your hands thoroughly after handling it.

Kiln Safety

Kilns specially designed for firing metal clay are efficient and well insulated but the back, sides, and top still get very hot during the firing process. Take this into consideration when choosing a place to set up your kiln. Keep the back and sides at least 12 inches (30.5cm) away from walls and other objects, and allow plenty of clear space over the top of your kiln, too (the top will get hot enough to burn your hand if you touch it during the firing). The bottom of a metal clay kiln is insulated, so it's safe to place it on any surface. I've fired my kiln on a kitchen counter, a wooden table, and a washing machine without experiencing any problems. Leave enough room to one side of the kiln for a heat-resistant surface next to it. I use a layer of brick on the countertop at the right side of my kiln because I'm right-handed; the kiln door opens to the left, making loading and unloading hot kiln shelves safer. Be sure to read the special instructions about when to vent your kiln in the section on Using Burnout Materials, page 41.

Butane torch and tripod soldering stand

THE TORCH: HEAT IN A HURRY

A butane kitchen torch, sometimes called a crème brûlée torch, can be used to fire small quick- or medium-fire pieces one at a time. These should be no larger than 1 inch (2.5 cm) in diameter or greater than ⅛ inch (3 mm) thick. The acetylene or propane torches used by jewelers also can be used. Be aware that these types of torches are all capable of temperatures higher than metal clay can take, so it's possible to accidentally melt the silver.

Torch Safety

Read and follow the manufacturer's guidelines before using your torch for the first time. Set the metal clay on a soldering pad, which you've placed on a tripod soldering stand, at least 4 inches (10.2 cm) above the work surface. Metal clay suppliers sell torch kits that come with a torch, stand, soldering pad, and directions. A convenient place to do your torch firing is on top of your kitchen stove. It was designed to handle high heat and you can turn on your

Judy Kuskin. *Untitled,* 2002. Largest rectangle: 2 x 1¼ x ⅛ in. (5 x 3.2 cm x 3 mm). Polymer clay, silver metal clay; painted metal clay paste; embedded in polymer clay after firing. PHOTO BY ARTIST.

overhead exhaust to draw away the smoke from the binder. The smoke is not dangerous (the binder is nontoxic); it just smells like burnt toast.

The Work Space

Setting up your metal clay work space is easy and affordable. I started working with metal clay at my kitchen table. This may be where you get started, too. Metal clay is safe and nontoxic, so working in the kitchen is fine, but it's better not to reuse kitchen items for food preparation. Your work space should be free of drafts or the clay will dry out as you're working it.

If you're as fond of tools and gadgets as I am, you'll eventually want enough space to sprawl. Now I work on a bench topped with a piece of white kitchen countertop in my converted-garage studio. My bench is 96 inches (2.4 m) long and 30 inches (76.2 cm) deep. Half of the bench is set up for working with unfired metal clay; the other, for finishing and other postfiring work. I like working on a laminated plastic countertop because it's easy to wipe down at the end of the day. I have two adjustable-arm desk lamps, bolted to either end of the bench, that I can swing to just the right spot. I don't work with a magnifying visor, as some metalsmiths and crafts people do, but they're handy, and someday my eyes will need the added magnification. My studio doesn't have running water, but I haven't found it to be a limitation to working with metal clay. Keep on hand a gallon each of distilled water and tap water, a plastic wash basin, a spray bottle, and a water dish. To prevent muscle fatigue, set the height of your chair or stool so your elbows are working at 90-degree angles.

I also recommend keeping a fire extinguisher suitable for electrical equipment (in the United States, these have a rating of "C") close by, in plain view, and easily accessible. Your local fire company will be happy to give you a lesson on how to use a fire extinguisher.

If you have a kiln, put it on a stable surface. Allow enough room to one side of the kiln for a heat-resistant surface (I use a layer of brick on the countertop). Arrange the area so unloading the hot kiln shelves will be safe and simple.

Finally, gather together the supplies listed for the Basic Toolbox on pages 14–17, as well as any additional tools listed for the project you intend to make. You're ready to get started.

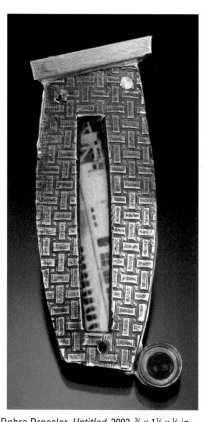

Debra Dressler. *Untitled,* 2002. ¾ x 1½ x ⅛ in. (1.9 x 3.8 cm x 3 mm). Silver metal clay; textured, patinated, sterling silver bezel, sterling silver square wire, mica, carnelian framing original photo by artist.
PHOTO BY ROBERT DIAMANTE.

Creating with Metal Clay

IF THERE ARE ANY RULES TO WORKING WITH METAL CLAY, the most important one is to keep the clay moist. Usually when you first open the new, tightly sealed package, it's the perfect working consistency. From this point on, though, you'll always be trying to return to this wonderfully balanced moisture content, which is essential for the best workability and performance. With lump clay, pinch off just enough for the project, then tightly cover the rest in plastic wrap. At the end of a work session, I wrap my clay in heavyweight plastic wrap, place it in a small reclosable plastic storage bag, then store this in a larger bag that holds a damp paper towel or a brand-new, damp sponge. I do this because I live in a dry climate. You may live in a more humid area, but if you work with metal clay only occasionally, I recommend this storage method for you, too. Metal clay never goes bad, either. One metal clay manufacturer stamps a date on the package. This isn't an expiration date, but simply a reference so you can use your oldest clay first.

Now you're ready to start handling the clay. To keep it from sticking to your hands, rub them with a little olive oil (or a hand balm with a high content of olive oil). Wipe down the work surface and rolling pin to keep the fine particles of metal clay from sticking to them as well. This layer of olive oil also helps slow down the drying process, but too much olive oil causes the clay to slip around like a greased pig. If this happens, use a paper towel to wipe the excess oil from your hands, tools, and work surface.

First test the moisture content of the clay (see photo 1). Squish a pea-size ball of lump clay between your fingers. If there are no cracks around the edges of the flattened ball of clay, it's the perfect consistency for working wet. If the clay needs a little more moisture, I will use the fine mist spray bottle to add distilled water to the lump form of metal clay, then knead it between some plastic food wrap. By kneading it in plastic, it keeps the clay from drying out further and keeps your fingers clean. After kneading the moisture into the clay, wrap the clay tightly in plastic wrap and allow it to sit for a few minutes, giving the water particles time to seep between the

Tim McCreight. *Untitled,* 2002.
1¼ x 1¼ x ⅛ in.
(3.1 x 3.1 cm x 3 mm).
Fine silver and flocking.
PHOTO BY ROBERT DIAMANTE.

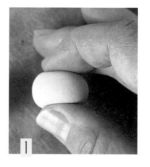

particles of binder and precious metal. When working with several separate clay pieces, keep them tented under heavyweight clear plastic food wrap until you're ready to join them.

Rehydrating

Though your goal should be to protect any unused portions from exposure to the air, it's reassuring to know that you can use the clay again and again. It's possible to recondition, or *rehydrate*, it from any state of dryness.

If the clay has dried out to the point that it cracks into separate pieces, it needs serious reconditioning. First, make some holes in the lump with the handle end of the blender tool, add distilled water, then allow enough time for the water to be absorbed. This could take a few hours or a few days, depending on the climate and the condition of the clay. Once the water is absorbed, knead the clay through heavyweight plastic food wrap.

Bone-dry metal clay must be chopped into tiny pieces before you add any water to it. I use a vegetable chopper for this process (see photo 2). Place the pieces in an airtight container, adding only enough distilled water to cover the pieces; set it aside for several days. When the pieces have absorbed the water, transfer the clay to plastic wrap. Alternate adding more water and kneading the clay. When the clay has nearly returned to its original consistency, add one drop of gel-type water-soluble glue and knead it again through the plastic wrap. Don't use too much glue or you'll have a sticky mess.

Making & Using Slip

The term *slip* comes from the ceramic world. Slip is simply a more liquid form of metal clay; it's so handy! Use it as a kind of glue, for filling gaps between parts before firing them, or for repairs after firing. Load slip into a syringe and use it as surface decoration, or trowel it on like plaster to create smooth or bumpy surface textures.

To make slip, flatten a pea-size ball of lump clay onto a rigid work surface. Mist the clay once, then work the water into the clay with the plastic pallet knife, as shown in photo 3. This process takes some time; don't add more water until you've completely worked the first spray of water into the clay. As the slip thickens, keep mixing it. A slight delay occurs before the water is absorbed into the binder and silver particles, but once this happens you'll notice the slip thinning out, even though you haven't added more water, as you continue to mix it (see photo 4). If you add too much water the slip will be soupy, so be patient as you work with the palette knife. (Let a too-wet slip sit uncovered for 10 to 20 minutes, then use the pallet knife to blend it together.)

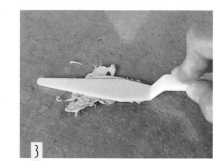

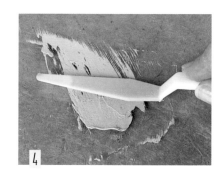

Designer Celie Fago keeps three slip containers—one for each of three different consistencies: thin, thick, and really thick. On the other hand, I prefer one consistency for repairs and for slip texture. I like to keep just one container of really thick slip, in the appropriate formula, handy at my work area. If I need thinner slip, I can dilute it at that time. To fill surface cracks that appear in unfired clay, I mix a thin slip to the consistency of heavy table cream. Use thick slip (the consistency of cake frosting) like glue to attach two pieces of unfired bone-dry clay to each other or as a texture material (for more information, see page 31). *Really* thick slip (the consistency of wall spackle) is good for making repairs in previously fired pieces. I'm careful to recycle metal clay, too. At the end of my metal clay workday I reclaim and add all the little scraps and filings from my work surface to my slip jar.

Working Wet

Many of the techniques for working with lump metal clay are implemented when the clay is moist or "wet." Cut moist clay into any shape, tear it for a loose edge, or poke holes for hanging cord or earring hooks. As with ceramic and polymer clays, you can press a texture into the metal clay surface and easily shape or model it. Assemble several modeled pieces together, push it into molds, create flat, two-dimensional pieces, or form it around a core to make three-dimensional designs. In this section you'll learn basic techniques for working with lump clay, slip, syringe, and paste.

Suz O'Dell. *Three Strand Biwa Pearl Necklace,* 2001. 26 in. (66 cm). Hand-built barrel screw clasp, slide, biwa pearls, silver metal clay and sterling silver wire. PHOTO BY GEORGE POST.

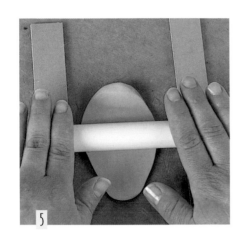

ROLLING IT FLAT

The most economical use of lump material is to roll it out to a sheet. Start with a ball of clay. Roll it tightly between the palms of your hands to eliminate any lines or pinches in the ball that might cause imperfections. Now flatten the ball onto the work surface, then put your choice of spacers—mat board or two stacks of playing cards—on either side of it. Use a lightly oiled rolling pin to roll out the clay, as shown in photo 5, much as you would roll out piecrust.

CUTTING SHAPES

Use a pin tool and a plastic drawing template to cut out geometric shapes in a variety of sizes (see photo 6). A craft knife works well for freehand shapes (see photo 7) and a tissue blade easily cuts a long straight line, as shown in photo 8. For some pieces you may like the natural edge created when you rolled out the clay. To make your own deckled edge, gently tear a flat piece of clay, holding your thumbs close together (see photo 9). Doing it this way lets you control the direction of the tear. The Natural brooch on page 111 uses this technique.

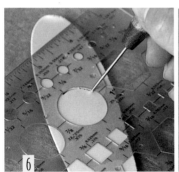
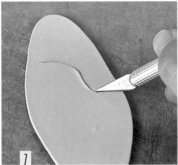
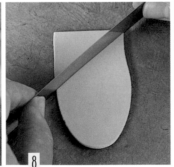
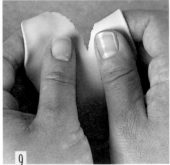

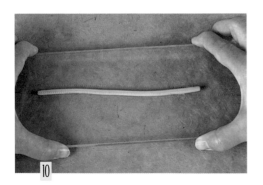

MODELING

Many of the projects in this book begin by using modeling—also known as sculpting or hand building—techniques. Three-dimensional designs often begin as simple coils and balls, the building blocks of design. Here's an easy trick I learned from the polymer clay community to make an even coil with the same diameter from end to end. Start by rolling the coil with your finger on a ¼-inch-thick (6 mm) piece of plate glass. Use another piece of glass to roll it out, as shown in photo 10 on page 28. This distributes equal pressure along the length of the coil and keeps it moist, reducing the risk of cracking.

MAKING HOLES

When it's moist, you can easily punch holes in the clay for places to hang earring wires, jump rings, added beads, or to slip a leather cord through the hole for a pendant. I keep a variety of plastic beverage straws and stirring sticks handy for this purpose. Simply use the straw like a cookie cutter, as shown in photo 11. For larger holes, use a circle pattern cutter. Remember to add the plug of moist metal clay back to the lump, or a dried-out one to your slip jar.

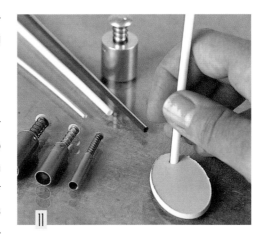

EMBOSSING

The first time you press an organic or manmade object into clay, the way you see the world will be forever transformed. You'll start noticing intriguing textures in every facet of your life. The cap on the toothpaste, the pattern on the spoon as you stir your morning coffee, the keys in your pocket—they'll all take on new meaning as you realize their creative potential. Soon you'll see exciting textures everywhere you look. I've found inspiration in a plastic mesh vegetable bag, a beverage cap, and a comb. Organic materials, such as sea shells, seed pods, corn husk, tree bark, or a bamboo sushi mat make a variety of elegant patterns that I am drawn to use over and over again in my work (see photo 12). Find unique textures in unlikely things such as the handle of a ladies' razor, a toothbrush, a metal typewriter ball, or a meat tenderizing mallet. Hardware stores are a treasure trove of textures, from the heads of nuts, bolts, and screws to the wide array of stuff found in all those little bins.

Some of my favorite textures and patterns are created from various shapes of mini pasta. I leave the piece to dry, then fire it with the pasta still in place, capturing the distinct and crisp

Mini-pasta makes great texture.

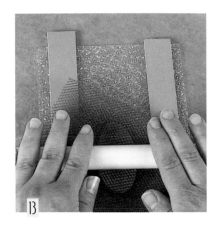

edge detail of the original material. Use this technique with any material that will burn out completely, including small pieces of fabric, like burlap and lace. See Using Burnout Materials on page 41 for special notes about firing precautions.

Use overlapping impressions from rubber stamps for a fun random pattern, or fashion your own stamping texture tools by altering plastic erasers, craft sticks, barbecue skewers, and plastic beverage stirrers. The marks in the Sparkling Squares pendant on page 80 and CeCe's Cornucopia earrings on page 65 came from tools I made. Finally, there are those great plastic texture sheets. Lay one on a rolled-out piece of metal clay then roll over it. You can even create a double-sided texture, as shown in photo 13.

WET TEXTURING

With commercially prepared paste, your own homemade slip, or a metal clay syringe, you can create wonderful "wet textures." From my experience teaching metal clay workshops, I find it interesting that everyone's slip and syringe textures are unique and individual in the same way handwriting is.

Thinned-Paste Texture

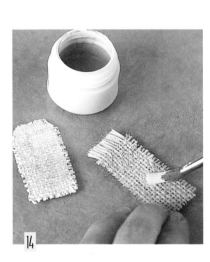

I was excited to discover that I could liquify metal clay paste enough to paint it on an organic object like a dry leaf or twig, or on textured fabric like burlap or lace. These materials then burn away in the firing process, leaving a hollow replica of the original form. The firing time is longer than the times recommended for other paste projects. Be sure to read about burnout materials on page 41, and also refer to the firing chart.

Multiple layers of thinned paste were painted over burlap, and the burlap burned away during firing.

Measure ¼ teaspoon (1 mL) of distilled water into a new jar of metal clay paste (it's sometimes easier to measure such a small amount of water by pulling it up into a clean syringe). Mix the paste well with a craft stick, being careful not to create bubbles as you stir. Let the mixture rest for 10 minutes, then give it another thorough stir. Now paint a thin layer of diluted metal clay paste directly on the organic object with a watercolor brush, as shown in photo 14. Allow the paste to dry (there is no rushing this method, so be patient). Repeat the process 10 to 12 times, stirring the paste before adding the next layer, because the silver particles settle to the bottom. The Twig & Leaf Condiment Spoon on page 137 shows the realistic rendering that is possible with this technique.

Slip Texture

By troweling a thick slip on bone-dry clay you can make wonderfully rich slip texture, as shown in photo 15. If you've ever frosted a cake, you're already familiar with this wet texturing technique. I don't recommend applying slip to moist clay; you might pick up bits of the underlying layer of metal clay as you work and cause rips or tears in it. You can repair these rips or tears, but you run less risk by working on a bone-dry piece. To find a texture you like, first practice troweling slip onto your rigid work surface.

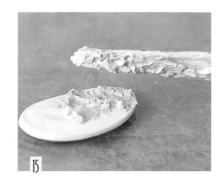

Extrusion Texture

This is a quick way to build up a thick, interesting texture from a pastelike form of metal clay that is sold in syringes. The syringe acts like a tiny caulking gun that pushes, or extrudes, a wormlike coil of the clay through a small opening at the end of the tool. Start by cutting off the end of the conical tip of the syringe; how much you cut from the end of the tip determines the diameter of the extruded clay. Remove the manufacturer's seal from the syringe itself, then attach the tip by turning it clockwise. Dampen a bone-dry piece of metal clay by brushing it with water. Hold the syringe ¼ inch (6 mm) above the surface, letting the extruded material fall onto it, as shown in photo 16. I used this technique for the Lacy Pearls earrings on page 54.

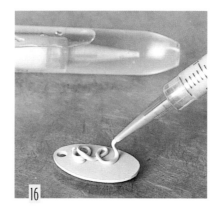

JOINING MOIST CLAY PIECES

Water activates the binder in metal clay, making it easy to stick pieces together. Lightly brush some on the two surfaces, allowing it to penetrate for a few seconds, then lightly press the two pieces together. If the pieces are small, set the smaller piece on the larger one, press them together, and brush the perimeter of the smaller piece with water (see photo 17). Wait a few minutes, then check to see if the seam is completely attached. If the smaller piece has pulled away, press that area again before brushing it with more water.

BLENDING SEAMS

To smooth adjoining edges of moist metal clay, you'll need to learn how to blend their seams. This simple technique results in multi-part pieces with greater strength and a very finished look.

Brush both sides of the seam with a little water, then use a blender tool or the back of your fingernail to smooth it until it disappears. Push the clay across the seam in two opposing directions; going in only one direction thins the clay too much on one side to make a strong enough joint. Then, when the piece is fired, the shrinking clay will open and crack there. Practice the technique by making a small band ring as a gift to yourself before making one of the larger projects with blended seams.

CREATING A HOLLOW CORE

Hollow-form designs, such as the Perfume Amphora on page 140, present an exciting new dimension in working with metal clay. This more advanced technique lets you make larger, lighter pieces. These are more comfortable to wear, and using a hollow core is also an economical way of using the clay.

You'll start with a core of combustible material such as paper, a wooden dowel, a piece of florist foam or a polystyrene form, ready-to-eat breakfast cereal—even a puffed cheese snack. These porous materials must first be covered with a smooth, thin layer of low-melt wax (beeswax or jeweler's wax works well) or fabric glue. This coating provides a smooth and slightly tacky surface for the clay to hold onto and, as it burns away, it creates an allowance space for the clay to shrink into. Pierce the core material with a barbecue skewer and use an inexpensive, disposable brush to apply at least two layers of wax or fabric glue, as shown in photo 18. Let the wax cool, then add a second coat, or if you're using fabric glue, let it dry overnight between coats.

For a form with a diameter of 1 inch (2.5 cm) or smaller, put the clay pieces directly on the wax- or glue-covered core. Blend the seams (see photos 19 and 20) and you're ready to add surface decoration. It's important to support a hollow design during firing, so nestle the form in a saucer of vermiculite or alumina hydrate.

Sometimes a form larger than 1 inch (2.5 cm) in diameter will collapse, or *slump*, during the critical sintering phase, when the piece is not yet solid. To avoid this problem you'll need to apply a support layer made of a substance that won't burn away during the firing, such as a special paper clay with volcanic ash added, then add another layer of wax or glue before putting on the clay itself. Barbara Simon created the very large Maltese Fish on page 39 using this additional support material.

MAKING & USING MOLDS

I've adapted press molding, a time-honored technique used in ceramic clay and in fine jewelry design, to metal clay. The commercially made molds for cookies, candy, butter, candles, and plaster are convenient, and these wonderful little shapes really excite your creative vision as you discover all the possibilities they offer.

For a clean release of the clay later, first coat the inside of the mold with a fine mist of olive oil before pressing the metal clay into it. Shape some moist lump clay into a slightly pointed cone (see photo 21). Press this end into the center of the mold, then use a flat, clear surface, such as a clear plastic lid, to finish pressing the clay into the mold, as shown in photo 22. You'll be able to see whether the clay has spread out to the edges and completely filled the mold (if not, pull it out, add a bit more clay, ball it all up, and try again). A well-filled mold also assures a good impression and reduces the risk of trapped air bubbles. If you want to capture the crispest, finest detail from the mold, let the metal clay dry in it.

Making Your Own Mold

Have you ever thought about how nice it would be to have one of your treasured childhood trinkets captured forever in solid silver or gold? I've found this an exciting realm of possibility—one with very few boundaries. You can make your own mold from virtually any object by using a two-part silicone mold compound, available through jewelry and hobby supply sources. Be sure to follow the manufacturer's safety recommendations, and don't let the silicone come in contact with rubber (for example, latex gloves), or you'll have a chemical reaction on your hands—literally!

This reusable silicone mold was made from a decorative button.

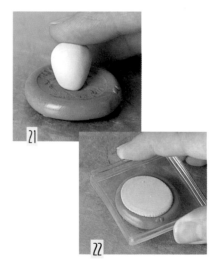

21

22

The compound solidifies when the two different-colored component materials combine. Knead equal portions of the compound together (see photo 23) until its color is uniform and shows no streaks. Press the original object into the soft, puttylike compound, as shown in photo 24. Allow the mold to cure; depending on the brand, this takes anywhere from 5 to 20 minutes. To test whether the compound is fully cured, press a tool into one side of it. If the tool leaves an indentation, the compound is not yet set. When it is, remove the object from the mold. Silicone molds don't need to be coated with olive oil as do commercial molds. The surface of the silicone is naturally slick and the metal clay releases easily without it.

WET REPAIRS

The most common problems—breaks, gaps, or cracks—that appear in moist metal clay are pretty simple to fix. Don't use water alone to repair a break in the material, because it won't work. Use a really thick slip made from the same clay formula as the piece itself. Use a blender tool to smooth the area.

Depending on how much time you've invested in the piece, sometimes it's better to ball up the clay and start again than to repair it. Chances are you'll make a better piece the next time.

DRYING WET CLAY

You're probably ready to see your work in gleaming silver or gold, but the piece must be bone dry before you fire it. Use this reliable test to determine whether it's ready or not. Lay the piece on the back of your hand or hold it to your cheek. If the piece feels cool (or even a bit clammy) it's not dry enough. It's very important that the clay be thoroughly dry. Otherwise, trapped moisture erupts into tiny surface blisters when you fire the clay. Here are two approaches to the drying process.

Air Dry

Air drying any metal clay project is a tried and true method, and a pretty safe way to work. If any part of your piece is 4 millimeters or more thick it's best to let the piece dry slowly, ideally overnight. Let air circulate all around the clay by putting it on a drying rack; this way it will dry faster than if you leave it on a work surface; see page 16 for more information about making a rack.

Applied Heat

Most of us are impatient to have our pieces finished. I know I am! Who wants to wait hours for a piece to dry, especially when the latest formula of metal clay fires in minutes? You can apply low, gentle heat to your project with a hair dryer. Use it at the lowest speed, and hold it at least 12 inches (30.5 cm) away, or lay it on a cup-warming plate. Don't forget to let the piece come to room temperature before checking to see if it's bone dry and ready to fire.

Working Dry

Certain design, refining, and repair processes ought to be done to bone-dry, rather than wet, metal clay.

REFINING EDGES

Smooth a rough edge by filing it with an emery board. Use a coarse grit first, then repeat the filing with a fine grit. File over a sheet of clean paper to save the powdered filings for your slip jar.

MAKING HOLES

Drill into the bone-dry clay with a drill bit glued into the end of a dowel rod. Twist the drill bit in only one direction (see photo 25), but don't press too hard or the piece will break. If you're very careful you also can use a flexible-shaft motor tool. Be sure to use a block of wood to support the metal clay piece, and wear eye protection.

CARVING

Carving is a great way to add pattern and texture to original-formula metal clay (the newer formulas don't cut as cleanly at bone-dry stage; they tend to crumble instead). Use a linoleum carving tool, and try a few of the many nib designs, each of which creates a different line quality.

It's easier to carve dry metal clay than a linoleum block. To get accustomed to the correct pressure needed for carving, practice first: Sacrifice a little slow-firing clay to the carving gods. Sketch

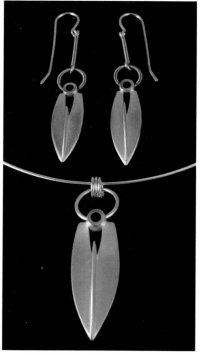

Terry Kovalcik. *Finned Arrow*, 2001. Pendant: 1⅜ x ½ x ½ in. (3.5 x 1.3 x 1.3 cm); earrings: 1¼ x ⅜ x ⅜ in. (3.2 cm x 9.5 x 9.5 mm). Silver metal clay; sterling silver findings, and polymer inlay.
PHOTO BY CORRIN KOVALCIK.

your design onto a piece of ⅛-inch-thick (3 mm) bone-dry clay with a graphite pencil; it will burn away later. Start with a shallow, 22° angle, and a #1 tip to carve away only a small amount of material (see photo 26). Begin carving in the center of the design before moving to the edges; ease your pressure on the tool as you get close to an edge, or you could crack the piece. If this happens, it's best to start again. (Chop it up into small pieces to use for slip. Nothing is wasted in working with metal clay.) To get a deeper groove, increase the angle to 45° and go back over the design but don't carve the clay more than twice or you may break through it. If that happens, roll another layer of the same clay to the thickness of two playing cards. Moisten both surfaces, then add the new layer to the back. Let the clay become bone dry before carving it again.

BUILDING WITH SLABS

You can create flat-sided designs, such as boxes and earrings, from bone-dry slabs of metal clay. First, carefully make a mockup with pieces cut from an index card; this will become the pattern for accurately cutting the pieces from rolled-out clay. When the parts are bone dry, glue them together with small dabs of water-soluble gel-type glue. Once the glue is dry, run a bead of metal clay from a syringe along all the inside seams (see photo 27). Smooth out all the seams with a blending tool; this action pushes the bead of clay into the seams from the inside and so the outside seams stay clean and attractive. I made the Fancy Filigreed Box (page 135) with this technique.

DRY REPAIRS

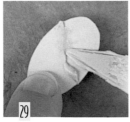

Slip is wonderful fixer-upper stuff. Even though it's disappointing to see a flaw in a fired piece, it's easy to fill a crack with thick slip using a plastic pallet knife. Smooth the seam or crack with a blender tool; dry it, fire it, then use a needle file to remove the extra metal. You can even reattach broken pieces by using slip the way you'd use glue (see photos 28 and 29). Whatever the repair job, use more slip than you need, then remove the excess after it's fired.

Stone Setting

Setting stones into metal clay may just be the quickest, easiest stone setting in the history of jewelry making. One basic principle: Be sure to allow enough space so the metal clay shrinks, traps the stone, and holds it securely in place. For original-formula metal clay, the stone should sit below the surface ⅛ inch (3 mm). The younger, quicker-firing metal clays shrink less, so set the stone a mere ¹⁄₁₆ inch (1.6 mm) below the surface. You'll probably find that one or two of your early stone-setting attempts pop out of the metal clay during firing. If it happens, you'll have a little more experience to help guide you the next time.

LAB-GROWN STONES

Laboratory-grown corundum, spinel, and stones in the cubic zirconia family are created under high heat and pressure and survive the firing process unscathed. Metal clay suppliers have tested a wide range of these laboratory-made stones, so I suggest that you purchase your stones from them. Otherwise, be warned—you're taking a risk. Stones can fracture—and even explode—during firing. It's not uncommon to quickly cool a hot piece of metal by *quenching* (plunging it into a water bath), but never quench metal clay pieces set with stones; they can't handle the sudden temperature change. You can safely finish stone-set pieces with a brass-bristle brush or with stainless steel shot, though. Those babies are tough!

NATURAL GEMSTONES

Natural semiprecious stones, such as turquoise and opals, or organic materials, like pearls and shells, can't withstand the heat of the kiln. Attach these materials after all the firing has been done. Refer to one of the many jewelry how-to books for information on setting semiprecious and precious gems using cold-connection jewelry-making techniques. Don't ever fire diamonds with metal clay. Diamonds can't withstand the heat, and as they burn up they become gray and cloudy.

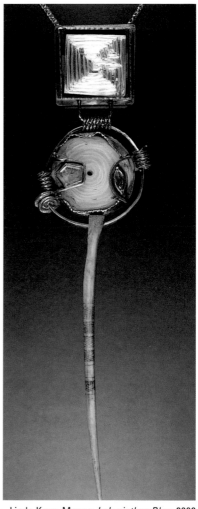

Linda Kaye-Moses. *Labyrinthos Blue,* 2000. Pendant: 7½ x 2¾ x 1½ in. (19 x 7 x 3.8 cm). Silver metal clay; sterling silver, tourmaline, bone, and handmade glass by S. Maddelena. PHOTO BY EVAN SOLDINGER.

HOW TO SET STONES

Setting a stone involves creating a *bezel,* a collarlike ring or band of metal, that holds the stone permanently in place. I'll demonstrate several setting styles that were used for various projects.

Ball Setting

Here's a nice, smooth bezel design. Roll a ball of metal clay with a diameter at least twice the depth of the stone itself. Brush the setting area with a light amount of water, set the ball in place, as shown in photo 30, then flatten it slightly with a clear plastic lid. Use a sharpened pencil to pierce a conical hole at the center of the flattened ball (refer to the illustration on page 82), or cut a hole with a drinking straw, as shown in photo 31. Set the stone with tweezers (as shown in photo 31), then press it ⅛ inch (3 mm) below the surface with the end of a beverage stirrer.

Syringe Setting

Cut a hole through the metal clay. Extrude a coil of metal clay from a syringe around the lip of the opening, as shown in photo 32. Set the stone into the opening, pressing it down ¹⁄₁₆ inch (1.6 mm) below the top surface of the syringe coil. This keeps the stone in place despite the shrinkage.

Layered Sheet Setting

I like this design because it has a fancy-shaped cutout setting, and the small hole behind the stone lets light shine through, beautifully illuminating it. Roll a small amount of medium- or quick-fire metal clay to the thickness of three playing cards. Cut out the shape; this will be the top layer that holds the stone. Cut a hole in this piece that is only ¹⁄₁₆ inch (1.6 mm) larger than the stone. Cut another shape, larger than the first, for the backing layer. Make a hole in this piece that is ⅛ inch (3 mm) smaller than the diameter of the stone. With a damp paintbrush, moisten the top of the backing layer and the underside of the top layer. To assure a good seam, press the layers together lightly, then wet their edges. Now there's a shelf for the stone. Set the stone in the opening (see photo 33).

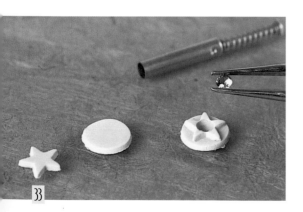

Syringe Lip Setting

Use this technique to set round or oval stones. Start by balling up a pea-size piece of medium- or quick-fire clay, then flatten the pea between your fingers to a ¼ inch (6 mm) thickness. Use a pattern cutter that is ¼ inch (6 mm) larger than your stone. Make a hole in the center of the punched piece with a drinking straw. Once the piece is bone dry, use a craft knife to trim away enough material to set the stone into the hole. Carve away only a little material at a time, checking the fit often. Once you have a tight fit, create a bezel lip by extruding a coil ⅛ inch (3 mm) below the clay's surface (see photos 34 and 35). Set the stone on the lip.

Firing

Tim McCreight, the metal-clay guru, is fond of pointing out that all forms of the clays may be fired with a torch, but the hard part is finding someone to hold a torch for two hours. No metal clay may be fired hotter than 1,650°F (900°C) for silver or 1830°F (1000°C) for gold. No matter which formula you use, longer firing times only make the metal stronger and more durable. Using a too-hot temperature, on the other hand, means disaster—doing so can melt your silver or gold.

Several factors will help you decide whether to use a torch or a kiln. A torch is just right for small objects—no thicker than ⅛ inch (3 mm) or larger than 1 inch (2.5 cm) in diameter—that were made with one of the two shorter-firing formulas. Use a kiln if any part of your piece was made with slow-fire metal clay, if you're firing a larger object, or when you'd like to fire several objects at the same time. And if your piece has elements made with more than one formula, *step down* the firing, so you can fire it at the longest time and lowest temperature possible.

KILN FIRING

I love the programmability of the kilns that are specially designed for metal clay because I can set it and forget it. If you use a small ceramics test kiln and a pyrometer, on the other hand, you'll have to carefully tend to the firing process. Start the timing only after the

Barbara Becker Simon. *Maltese Fish,* 2001. 2¼ x 1¾ x ¾ in. (5.6 x 4.4 x 1.9 cm). Hollow-formed silver clay; syringe embellishment, synthetic corundum, golden sapphire.
PHOTO BY ROB STEGMANN.

Barbara Becker Simon. *Lotus Leaf Pendant,* 1999.
1⅝ x 2 x ⅜ in. (4.1 x 5 cm x 9.5 mm). Champlevé
enamel in silver metal clay; lampworked beads by
the artist, glass beads, and pearls.
PHOTO BY LARRY SANDERS.

kiln has reached the recommended temperature. Either way, all formulas of metal clay may be fired in a kiln.

Load your kiln when it's at room temperature. The firing chart, below, gives recommended time/temperature information. Once the firing cycle is complete, let the heat escape by opening the kiln's door about 1 inch (2.5 cm). When the hot kiln is 400°F (204°C) or cooler you can safely remove a loaded shelf from the kiln. This also protects the kiln furniture from thermal shock, prolonging its life. A pair of heat-resistant gloves and a long-handled spatula, like the type used for outdoor grilling, make removing the shelves from the kiln safer. To quickly cool off a hot piece, pick it up with a pair of tweezers and quench it in water. Let a set-stone piece or one with enamel or glass air cool to room temperature. These materials are subject to fracturing if they're exposed to sudden temperature changes.

Inclusion Firing

An *inclusion* is any permanent element in your design that isn't made of metal clay but will be fired along with it. Because inclusion materials are usually more sensitive to heat, be sure to step down the firing; that is, lower the firing temperature and increase the firing time to compensate. You'll have to experiment in order to find the safe firing temperature for any unusual inclusion. With metal

		Kiln Firing Time (in minutes)				
		1	**10**	**20**	**30**	**120**
SLOW-FIRE	Gold					1,830°F (1000°C)
	Silver					1,650°F (900°C)
MEDIUM-FIRE	Silver		1,650°F (900°C)			
	Silver with sterling silver			1,560°F (850°C)		
	Silver with glass				1,470°F (800°C)	
QUICK-FIRE	Silver	1650°F (900°C)	1,290°F (700°C)			
	Silver with sterling silver			1,200°F (650°C)		
	Silver with glass				1,110°F (600°C)	

inclusion materials, such as sterling or 950 silver findings, or stones (mostly lab-grown ones), you can use a lower temperature and longer time. Be sure to refer to the firing chart on page 40 whenever you'll be using inclusions.

Please note that original-formula silver or gold metal clay must be fired at a single time/temperature combination that you can't step down. To use elements made from both newer-formula silver metal clay and slow-fire gold metal clay in a single piece, first fire the silver and gold parts separately, then join them with a bit of medium- or quick-fire lump silver metal clay (any form). Refire the piece for two hours; remember that the long firing time ensures that the added clay attains its optimum durability and creates the strongest possible bond between the previously fired silver and gold. I used this technique for the Folk Art Heart pendant on page 89.

Using Burnout Materials

There are certain times when it's very important to vent your kiln or fire the piece outdoors. Toxic gases may result when plastics, polystyrene, or combustible materials of unknown composition are burned. In addition, organic materials, combustible at temperatures ranging from 200°F to 500°F (93°C to 260°C), create a great deal of smoke as they combust, so be careful when you're firing anything organic along with the clay itself. Never open your kiln at this stage; the oxygen you introduce to the burning organic material can cause a flare-up and may burn you. Fire these designs longer than the times recommended for other medium-fire metal clay projects. I recommend setting the kiln at 1,650°F (900°C) and holding the piece at that temperature for 20 minutes.

TORCH FIRING

A torch is just right for firing small objects made with one of the shorter-firing formula metal clays. Because a torch doesn't have a temperature gauge, and most of them are hotter than needed for metal clay, you'll need to learn how to pay close attention to the transformation of the clay into metal. Otherwise, you might accidentally melt the piece. I suggest that you sacrifice a flattened pea-sized ball of unshaped clay in order to get some torch-firing expe-

Dawn Hale. *Mesopotamian Cylinder Seal Roll-Out Bracelet*, 2001. 1¼ x 3³⁄₁₆ x 2¼ in. (3.1 x 7.8 x 5.6 cm). 24k metal clay; diamonds, brass brushed, tumbled, and polished with rouge. PHOTO BY RALPH GABRINER.

36

37

38

39

40

41

experience. Learn how to recognize the four firing stages of metal clay before you fire a piece you've worked hard to design and execute.

Firing Stages

To begin, place a soldering pad on a metal soldering stand tripod that is at least 4 inches above the work surface. Light the torch and hold it a 45° angle to the piece. Concentrate the center of the flame at the edges of the piece and keep the torch moving; the heat will quickly move toward the center and you'll be using the fuel in the most efficient way. Carefully watch the character of the material as it goes through these stages, noticing especially the final color change that signals when the piece has turned to solid precious metal.

At *stage one*, the binder ignites and burns away (see photo 36). Once the piece starts to glow dimly red, it's at *stage two*, as shown in photo 37. At *stage three*, the piece glows brightly red (see photo 38). Hold the piece at this stage for the amount of time indicated below:

Medium-fire metal clay: hold for 5 minutes

Quick-fire metal clay: hold for 1 minute

Stage four is the critical point: The piece glows a brilliant red-orange and the surface is almost reflective (photo 39). Don't apply any more heat or the piece will begin to melt, first around the edges; the entire piece may well ball itself into a silvery puddle. If you do melt it, you can send the blob to a refiner to get the scrap value of the precious metal. This will be considerably less than the value of the metal clay you purchased. Be sure to tell the refiner that you're sending pure metal (999 FS or 24K gold).

Post-Firing Repairs

In my opinion, no piece is ever beyond repair. That's another great attribute of working with metal clay. Use a blender tool to fill cracks, gaps, holes, and blisters that appear after firing with thick slip, then fire the piece again. To repair a blister, file the area with a needle file before patching the hole, as demonstrated in photos 40 and 41.

Surface Finishing

When a silver clay piece comes from the kiln it's matte white rather than silver (see photo 42), and gold is a matte ocher color. This is because the surface is uneven and porous. If you could see a microscopic crosssection of the surface, it would look like a sponge. To achieve the finish that is usually associated with silver—be it shiny, satin, or highly polished—you'll burnish (compress) the metal's surface. Each project has a recommended finish using one of the basic jeweler's finishing techniques described below.

BURNISHED FINISHES

The wire-brushed satin finish, with its matte surface, has a wonderful luster that gently reflects light. It is the first step for any of the other burnished surface finishes described here.

Using liquid soap and running water, first scrub the piece with a wire brush made of fine brass bristles (see photo 43). The water and soap act as a lubricant for the scrubbing action. Never "dry brush" metal clay pieces, or you'll deposit bits of brass wire on the surface, making it look dirty and dull.

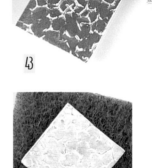

Soft Satin

This is a slightly more subtle, softer finish than a wire-brushed one. Start with a wire-brush finish, then scrub the surface with a new nylon scrubbing pad, using soap and running water (see photo 44).

Mirror

For this classic jewelry finish start with a wire-brush finish, then use a burnisher or a tumbler filled with stainless steel shot. The result is a high-polish, glossy shine (see photos 45 and 46). The advantage of using a handheld burnishing tool is that you can selectively high-polish specific areas, such as the high spots in a relief motif, as an eye-catching contrast to other areas with a more matte finish.

An even, high polish on silver or gold is a job for an electric tumbler, such as the type used by jewelers. The tumbler is filled with various sizes and shapes of stainless steel shot and a liquid burnishing compound. A great advantage to this is that you can tumble-

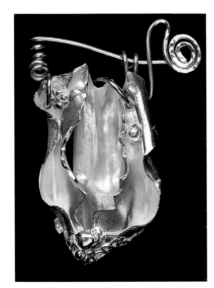

Mary Ann Devos. *Pearl in a Wave,* 2000. 2 x 1 x ¼ in. (5 x 2.5 cm x 6 mm). Hand-brushed finished silver clay; freshwater pearl, 24k gold accents, and sterling silver fibula. PHOTO BY ROBERT STEGMAN.

polish several pieces at once. As they tumble, I check my pieces every 20 minutes; don't let them go for more than 45 minutes—you might erode their textural surfaces. Follow the manufacturer's instructions for diluting the burnishing compound, and always keep the shot either completely dry or totally submerged in diluted burnishing compound. It's possible to ruin the shot, and it's expensive to replace.

Creating Patinas

Once the surface finish is complete, consider using a chemical coloring process, or *patina* (sometimes called antiquing), to color your silver or gold metal clay object. A wide range of metal colors is possible with this method. One of the most versatile and easily obtained patina solutions uses *liver of sulfur* (sulphurated potash). Use it to achieve a rainbow of colors on silver. Liver of sulfur is sold in liquid or lump form, and it's often available through bead shops, as well as where jewelers' supplies are sold. I get the best results with the lump form; I mix it as I need it, varying the concentration of the solution to obtain results I like.

Liver of sulfur patinas can range from pale gold to jet black.

Note: Be careful when using this chemical. Use stainless-steel tweezers to dip your piece in the solution, which only lasts for several hours. I recommend that you mark a glass or plastic container to hold the mild chemical solution and a separate one for the rinse water. Flush these into the septic system when you've finished. Recycle the containers or reuse them, but only for more patination.

APPLICATION

Place one pea-size lump of solid liver of sulfur in a glass or plastic bowl. Add one cup of the hottest water you can get from the tap. Let the lump dissolve; it will smell like rotten eggs and the water will turn a bright yellow-green color. Fill another glass or plastic bowl with cold water for the rinse.

Start with a piece that's clean and free of grease or oil (even the oil from your hands resists the patina). Grip the metal with the tweezers, swishing it in the solution for about two seconds, then dip the piece in the rinse water, as shown in photo 47. Reposition the tweezers and put the piece into the solution until you get the color you like. When you're happy with the results, hold the piece under cold running water for one minute (if the piece is hollow, such as a bead, it may be necessary to rinse it in fresh water to remove the solution from the inside of the form).

Each successive dip in the solution turns the silver metal clay a new color, from golden yellow to rose to a glowing magenta. After four dips in the liver of sulfur solution the patina is a red-violet; another dip turns it blue-purple, then steel blue. Finally, the patina goes to gray, blue-gray, then blue-black, a color I find interesting for its richness and depth. To continue further the patina will become jet black. I recommend that if you'd like a black patina, develop it slowly, rinsing between each color. If you plunk the piece in the liver of sulfur solution and let it sit there without rinsing in between color changes, the black can build up too quickly and may later flake off.

The purpose of patina is to enhance the piece's beautiful texture; after coloring the metal use a polishing cloth to wipe the color from the high areas, bringing them back to silver. The lighter and brighter foreground contrasts nicely against its darker background. If you don't like the patina, it can easily be removed with a dip-and-rinse tarnish remover, silver polish, or a polishing cloth.

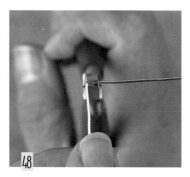

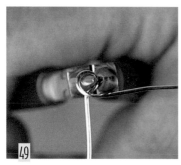

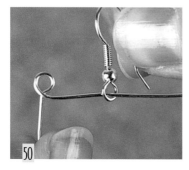

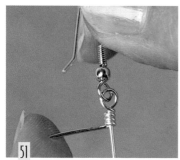

Making Jewelry Pieces

Now that you've learned all about what goes into making beautiful pendants, beads, earrings, and such, you'll want to be able to put it all together into great finished pieces. *Findings* are those clasps, ear wires, jump rings, and oddments that turn design elements into a piece of jewelry or wearable art. I think sterling silver or 18k gold ones are best; they'll do justice to your wonderful designs. To find out more about basic jewelry making techniques and tools, be sure to read one of the many great books dedicated to the jeweler's craft.

BASIC JEWELER'S WIRE WRAP

You'll use this simple technique again and again. Use sterling wire to attach metal clay pieces to findings in order to build linked bracelets, anklets, necklaces, or belly chains. Well-crafted wire wrapping takes some practice, so I suggest you first make some trial wraps with copper wire. Here, the wrap is used to create a link to an earring wire; it works equally well with many other findings.

With a pair of flat-nose pliers, bend the wire into a 90° angle, 1½ inches (3.8 cm) from the end of the wire, as shown in photo 48. Use round-nose pliers to clamp the wire ¼ inch (6 mm) from the bend, rolling the pliers toward the bend to make a loop (see photo 49). Thread the earring wire onto the loop (see photo 50). Wrap the remaining tail of wire three times around the stem wire (see photo 51). Use wire cutters to trim the extra wire as close to the stem wire as possible, then tightly clamp this end against the stem wire, using the flat nose-pliers.

ATTACHING A PIN BACK

A pin-back set consists of the sharp pin stem, a catch that holds the stem's sharp tip, and the joint that holds the stem's blunt end. You can purchase an inexpensive pin-back set that already has the parts soldered onto a small mount. This type of finding is glued to the piece with a two-part epoxy. It's quick and easy. Another, more polished method uses a sterling silver catch and joint, which are "soldered" directly to the piece with bits of medium-fire clay.

On the back of the pin, add two pea-size amounts of syringe metal clay, spacing the catch 1½ inches (3.8 cm) apart from the joint. Press the catch and joint into the moist clay. Use the blender tool to bring some material over the joint and onto the sides of the catch. Allow the clay to dry to bone dry.

Place the pin facedown on the kiln shelf. Since the pin set is made of sterling silver, you must step down the temperature. Fire the piece at 1,560°F (850°C) for 20 minutes. Allow it to air cool. Insert the nickel pin stem into the joint. Make sure the rivet is properly aligned before closing the joint with flat-nose pliers.

WITHIN EACH SECTION OF JEWELRY TYPES, the easiest projects come first. The Sculptural Pieces, in the last section, all use more challenging techniques.

My hope is that the projects that follow inspire you, the metal clay artist, to create many wonderful things. The history of metal clay is still young, and we are just beginning to discover the potential of this amazing medium, so have fun being a part of history in the making.

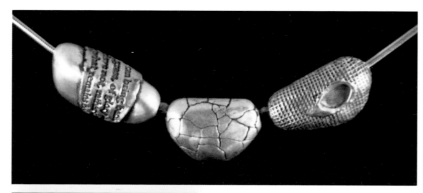

Hadar Jacobson. *Hollow Pebbles Necklace,* 2002. Beads: 1½ x 1 x ¼ in. (3.8 x 2.5 cm x 6 mm). Hollow-formed silver metal clay. PHOTO BY ARTIST.

Hadar Jacobson. *Window Hollow Ring,* 2001. ½ x 1¼ x 1¼ in. (1.3 cm x 3.2 cm x 3.2 cm). Hollow-formed silver metal clay. PHOTO BY ARTIST.

Silver Snails

Organic forms, especially those from the ocean, inspire some of my favorite motifs.

Tools & Materials

.3 ounce (8.4 g) medium-fire silver metal clay

Syringe quick-fire metal clay

See-through ruler or sheet of plate glass with finished edges

Craft knife

Sterling silver ear posts with 2-mm diameter pad

Tumbler with stainless steel shot

Instructions

1 Start a coil of medium-fire metal clay with your fingers, then use the plate glass to finish rolling it to ⅛ inch (3 mm) in diameter and 8 inches (20.3 cm) long. With the craft knife, cut the coil in half. Tent one under plastic wrap to keep it from drying out.

2 Taper one end of the coil, then roll it into a tight clockwise spiral. Brush water on the spiral's seam. To make sure the seam seals itself along the entire length of the spiral, slightly flatten the design with the glass. Repeat the process to make a counterclockwise coil. (If you twist both coils in the same direction you'll have two left-sided earrings or two right-sided ones. Hey, it's not like it's happened to me! If it does happen, make two sets of spiral earrings, one for you and one for a friend.) Let the earrings dry to bone dry.

3 Place the spirals on a kiln shelf and fire them at 1,650°F (900°C) for 10 minutes.

4 When the pieces cool, add the earring backs. Use the syringe to dab a 1/8-inch (3 mm) bit of quick-fire metal clay to the center of the spirals. Press the earring post into the fresh clay. Allow the clay to dry again and fire the earrings on a kiln shelf, front side down. You'll need a strong bond, so fire the finished earrings at 1,110°F (600°C) for 2 hours. The earring posts are made of sterling silver, so step down the firing temperature and lengthen the firing time or the sterling will melt. Paint the posts with silver clay slip prior to firing it so they won't oxidize.

5 When the pieces are cool, wire-brush with soap and water. To get a mirror finish, tumble them for 25 minutes.

Swaying Hearts

The heart is an eternal symbol of love. Send subtle signals with these swaying symbols of your affection.

Instructions

1. Use mat-board spacers to roll out a marble-size ball of clay to $\frac{1}{16}$ inch (1.6 mm) thick on top of one of your chosen textured surfaces. Press the other texture lightly on the top surface of the clay. I used plastic texture sheets available from professional polymer clay suppliers.

2. Move the clay directly to your work surface. Cut out a heart shape with the mini heart-shape cookie cutter (or use figure 1 as a template). Repeat to make the other earring.

3. While the clay is still moist, use a beverage stirrer stick to cut a hole in each of the hearts. Be careful not to cut the hole too close to the edge.

4. When the clay is bone dry, file the edges. Use a coarse emery board first, then a fine one.

5. Fire the hearts flat on a kiln shelf, close to one another but not touching, for two hours at 1,650°F (900°C).

6. First wire brush the silver, then tumble it for 20 minutes. Use liver-of-sulfur patina to create a blue-purple color, and polish the silver with a polishing cloth to remove the patina from the high points.

7. To assemble the components, review the Jeweler's Basic Wire Wrap on page 46. Add a bead to each earring assemblage then wire wrap both ends. Finish by adding the ear wires.

Tools & Materials

.1 ounce (2.8 g) slow-fire lump silver metal clay

Two different textured surfaces

Mini heart-shape cookie cutter, or use figure 1 template at 100%

Plastic beverage stirrer

Coarse and fine emery boards

Tumbler with stainless steel shot

Liver of sulfur

Polishing cloth

20-gauge sterling silver wire, 8 inches (20.3 cm) long

Wire cutters

Flat-nose pliers

Round-nose pliers

2 size 10° beads

Sterling silver French ear wires

Figure 1

Groovy Flowers

Tap into '60's flower power with these sweet and girlish earrings. The Groovy Flower Motif, featuring brightly shining cabochons, is also used to make a matching bracelet and ring.

Instructions for Groovy Flower Motif

The motif uses the layered sheet stone setting method.

1. On a flexible work surface, roll out metal clay to the thickness of three playing cards.

2. Use the pattern cutters to cut a flower shape, then cut a ³⁄₁₆-inch (5 mm) circle in its center.

3. Cut a ½-inch (1.3 cm) backing circle from the clay.

4. Moisten one side of the ½-inch (1.3 cm) circle and one side of the flower with water. With the damp sides together, press them lightly together. Also wet the edges to assure a good seam.

5. Use the stirrer to cut a hole in the backing circle. The diameter of the stirrer must be smaller than the ³⁄₁₆-inch (5 mm) circle cutter in order to create a shelf for the stone. The small hole behind the stone allows light to illuminate it.

6. Brush water around the top hole punched in the flower and set the stone in the center.

7. When the motif is bone dry, peel it from the flexible work surface.

Instructions for Earrings

1. Make two Groovy Flower Motifs. Fire them, lying flat on a kiln shelf, at 1,650°F (900°C) for 10 minutes and allow them to cool.

Tools & Materials

.1 ounce (2.8 g) medium-fire lump silver metal clay
Quick-fire syringe silver metal clay
Playing cards
Flower-shape cutter, ⁷⁄₁₆ inch (1.1 cm)
Circle cutter, ³⁄₁₆ inch (5 mm)
Circle cutter, ½ inch (1.3 cm)
Plastic beverage stirrer, smaller than ³⁄₁₆-inch (5 mm) diameter
2 pink sapphire cabochon laboratory-grown corundum, ³⁄₁₆ inch (5 mm) diameter
Sterling silver ear posts with 2-mm diameter pad
Alumina hydrate
Tumbler with stainless steel shot

2. Apply a ⅛-inch (3 mm) dab of quick-fire syringe metal clay to the back of the earrings, just above the hole for the stone. Press the earring post into the fresh clay. Allow the clay to dry.

3. Lay the earrings, stone side down, in a ⅛-inch (3 mm) bed of alumina hydrate on a kiln shelf. The earring posts are made of sterling silver, so you must step down the firing temperature or the sterling will melt. For the strongest bond, fire at 1,110°F (600°C) for two hours. Paint the earring post with silver clay slip prior to firing it. This protects the sterling silver from oxidization during firing.

4. Wire brush the earrings with soap and water to burnish them to a satin finish. Tumble the earrings for 25 minutes.

Lacy Pearls

These fancy earrings show how beautiful a mirror finish looks against unfinished, fired metal clay. The pearl drops make them extra dressy.

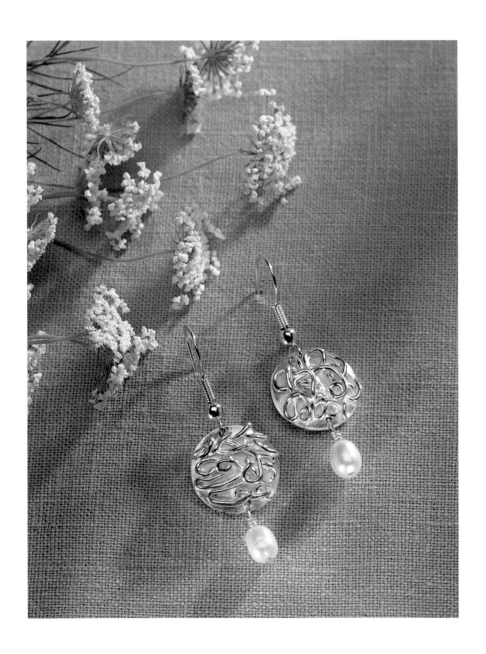

Instructions

Simultaneously firing the two clay formulas, which have different shrinkage rates, creates an interesting effect. The extruded syringe clay causes the earring's original circle shape (which is made of high-shrinkage, slow-fire clay) to draw itself into a dome.

1 Roll out the metal clay with mat-board spacers to ¹⁄₁₆ inch (1.6 mm) thick.

2 Trace around the nickel with the pin tool. Repeat to make the other earring. Poke holes at the top and bottom of each circle but don't get too close to the edge.

3 Let the circles dry to bone dry, then sand their edges with the coarse, then the fine, emery boards.

4 Brush the bone-dry circles with water to make the surface damp. Holding the syringe ¼ inch (6 mm) above the surface, let the extruded clay fall onto it (see figure 1). Keep the tip of the syringe in a cut-flower vial filled with ¼ inch (6 mm) water. Let the clay become bone dry.

5 Dust a ⅛-inch (3 mm) layer of alumina hydrate on a kiln shelf and place the earrings face up in the powder. Fire them at 1,650°F (900°C) for 2 hours.

6 Finish the earrings with a wire-brushed satin finish, then tumble them with stainless steel shot for 20 minutes. The earring circles remain frosty white, contrasting nicely with the mirror finish on the extruded decoration.

7 Add the ear wires to the disks. Thread the pearls onto the headpins. Create the loops, as shown in photos 48 and 49 on page 46, thread the disks into the looped wires, then finish with the wire wraps (see photos 50 and 51).

Tools & Materials

.2 ounce (5.6 g) slow-fire lump silver metal clay

Medium-fire syringe metal clay

A nickel or a circle template, ³⁄₈ inch (9.5 mm) diameter

Pin tool

Coarse and fine emery boards

Alumina hydrate

Tumbler with stainless steel shot

Sterling silver headpins

2 freshwater pearl beads

Flat-nose pliers

Round-nose pliers

2 sterling silver French ear wires

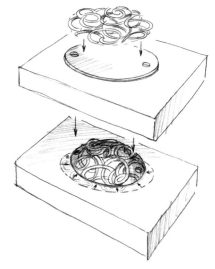

Figure 1

Ashanti

The bold geometric pattern creates an illusion of depth and movement in these swingy, lightweight earrings.

Instructions

1. Use mat-board spacers to roll out the metal clay to 1/16 inch (1.6 mm).

2. Use the plastic template and pin tool to cut two oval shapes from the clay.

3. Cut a hole with the stirrer near the top center of each oval; use the width of the stirrer to help you place it a safe distance from the edge.

4. Once they're bone dry, use the ruler to help you draw intersecting vertical and horizontal lines on the ovals (the graphite will burn away during the firing). Starting at the center, draw the diagonal lines.

5. Review the carving directions on pages 35–36. Using the linoleum carving tool, carve out the pattern in the same order that you drew it.

6. To make a well-matched pair, place the ovals with their carved sides facing each other and sand both their edges with first the coarse, then the fine, emery boards.

7. Make the metal clay accent beads. Roll the clay between your fingers to make two pea-size balls, then flatten them to 1/4-inch (6 mm) in diameter.

8. Use the stirrer to cut a hole in the center of each bead. Allow the metal clay beads to dry to bone dry.

Tools & Materials

.1 ounce (2.8 g) slow-fire lump silver metal clay

Oval template, 3.5 mm x 1.5 mm

Pin tool

Plastic beverage stirrer

See-through ruler

Linoleum carving tool

Coarse and fine emery boards

Liver of sulfur

2 accent beads, 3/16 inch (5 mm) diameter

2 sterling silver eye pins

2 sterling silver French ear wires

9. Fire the pieces lying flat on the kiln shelf at 1,650°F (900°C) for 2 hours.

10. Wire brush the surface, then apply liver of sulfur to blue-black. Polish the earrings with a polishing cloth so the blue-black remains only in the recessed carved areas.

11. Thread a carved earring, metal clay accent bead, and a 3/16 inch (5 mm) bead onto an eye pin, then follow the instructions in steps 19–21 on page 67.

Fire & Smoke

Fired in a simple raku
"kiln," these glazed
earrings capture the
action of fire and
smoke for an
exciting organic finish.

Instructions

There are a variety of commercially prepared raku glazes available from ceramic supply shops. I've tried several different colors and have had success with all of them. These glazes are typically sold in powder form and you must mix them just before using them. Be sure to follow the manufacturer's safety recommendations for handling the fine powder.

1. On a flexible work surface, use mat-board spacers to roll out the metal clay to 1/16 inch (1.6 mm) thick.

2. Use the pin tool and the circle template to cut two 1½-inch (3.8 cm) circles.

3. Use the craft knife to cut a 7/16-inch (1.1 cm) square with rounded edges in the center of a circle. (Sharp-cornered openings cause the metal clay to crack in the drying stage.) Repeat for the other circle.

4. Roll out six tiny balls of clay. Make each one slightly different in size. Dimple the clay circles with the end of a paintbrush, three on each earring, where you would like to attach the balls. Brush the dimples with water and press the clay balls lightly into them.

5. Poke a hole with the pin tool at the top of each circle, rotating it to enlarge the opening slightly.

6. When the clay is bone dry, sand the edges with the coarse emery board.

Tools & Materials

.3 ounce (8.4 g) slow-fire lump silver metal clay

Pin tool

Circle template, 1½ inches (3.8 cm) diameter

Craft knife

Square template with 7/16-inch (1.1 cm) opening

Watercolor paintbrush

Commercial raku glaze

Coarse emery board

Plastic container with a tight-fitting lid

Four kiln blocks

10 inches (25.4 cm) of 22-gauge brass wire

10 inches (25.4 cm) of 20-gauge steel wire

Standard kiln brick, cut to 4 x 4 x 2½ inches (10.2 x 10.2 x 6.4 cm) with a hacksaw

Large, 32-ounce (.9 kg) tin can

Newspaper

Old cookie sheet

Metal pot lid

Brick, or similar weight

Matches

Heat-resistant gloves

Long-handled tweezers

2 sterling silver French ear wires

7. Fire the piece flat on a kiln shelf at 1,650°F (900°C) for 2 hours.

8. In a small container with a tight-fitting lid, mix the glaze to the consistency of table cream. Shake the glaze mixture for one minute. Let it sit until the air bubbles come to the surface.

9   Raku firing involves smoke and open flame, so I suggest you move your cooled kiln outside or into a well-ventilated area to finish the earrings. Arrange the four kiln blocks in the corners on the floor of the kiln. Preheat the kiln to 1,500°F (816°C).

10   Hook the earrings onto a piece of brass wire. Stir the glaze to make sure it is evenly mixed and dip the earrings into the glaze. Hang them to dry, then dip them again in the well-mixed glaze.

11   Remove the earrings from the brass wire and hang them from two steel wire hangers. Secure wires in kiln brick, as shown in figure 1.

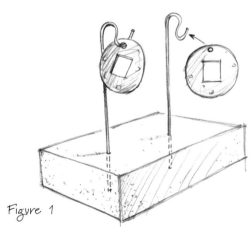

Figure 1

12   Fill the large tin can with shredded newspaper and put it on an old cookie sheet next to your kiln. Gather together a cool kiln shelf, a stack of folded wet newspaper, a metal pot lid, a brick (or something similar you can use as a weight), and a pack of matches.

13   Place the earrings on a kiln shelf and set the shelf in the kiln so it rests on the kiln blocks. When the kiln's temperature returns to 1,500°F, (816°C) check the glaze after three

minutes; open the kiln door just wide enough to see if the glaze is molten (wet and glassy-looking). If it isn't, close the door and check again in another minute.

14   Wear heat-resistant gloves to move the kiln brick onto the cool kiln shelf. Use the tweezers to remove the earrings, still on the hangers, from the brick and quickly drop them in the can. The newspaper should catch on fire. If it doesn't, toss in a lit match.

15   Once the newspaper is burning well, stack the wet newspaper, lid, and brick over the can's opening, as shown in figure 2. Let the newspaper burn until the oxygen in the can is depleted and the fire goes out (about 10 minutes). It's important to let the fire completely consume the oxygen in the can in order to achieve this beautiful and interesting raku glaze.

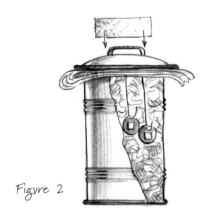

Figure 2

16   Remove the earrings from the newspaper ash and wash away the smoky residue with soap and warm water.

17   Attach the sterling silver ear wires to complete the earrings.

Simple Weave

These earrings, set with little jewels in an intricate woven pattern, dazzle the eye.

Instructions

1. Use the knife and ruler to cut the metal clay paper in half. From one of the halves, cut nine strips that measure ⅛ x 2⅜ inches (3 mm x 6 cm). From the remaining half, cut 19 strips, each ⅛ x 1¼ inches (3 mm x 3.2 cm).

2. Start weaving the clay strips from left to right: Lay down one vertical strip, then add the horizontal pieces, alternating over and under. Attach them securely to each other with a brush of water. Wait several minutes for the water to dry so the strips adhere to each other. (Securely attaching the first row makes the weaving easier. If water alone doesn't do the job, use a very small amount of clear gel-type water-soluble glue.) Weave the rest of the vertical strips into the horizontal ones, placing them as close as possible to each other. Attach the last vertical piece with the water-soluble glue. Let the glue dry.

3. Roll out the medium-fire metal clay to the thickness of three playing cards. Cut a 2½ x 1¼-inch (6.4 x 3.2 cm) rectangle. This will be slightly larger than the woven piece. Brush water on the surface.

4. Using a playing card, carefully lift the woven piece and place it on top of the plain rectangle. Lightly press the woven piece in place with your fingers. Let the piece become bone dry. Use a tissue blade to cut the rectangle into two 1⅛ x 1⅛-inch (2.8 x 2.8 cm) squares. Put the squares together with the faces touching. File the edges with a fine emery board.

5. Use the paper punch to punch holes in the bottom left and right corners. Set the stones with the syringe stone setting method, as described on page 38.

Tools & Materials

.2 ounce (5.6 g) metal clay paper

Syringe silver metal clay

.1 ounce (2.8 g) medium fire metal clay

Craft knife

See-through ruler

Watercolor paintbrush

Clear gel-type water-soluble glue

Playing cards

Tissue blade

Fine emery board

Paper punch with ⅛-inch (3 mm) diameter hole

2 sterling silver earring posts with 2-mm pad

2 cubic zirconia, ⅛ inch (3 mm) diameter

Size #0 blender tool

Liver of sulfur

Polishing cloth

6. Lay the earrings flat on a kiln shelf and fire them for 10 minutes at 1,650°F (900°C). Let the earrings air cool.

7. To attach the sterling silver earring posts, extrude a pea-size amount of clay to the center back of an earring. Press the earring back into the clay. Use the blender tool to bring some soft clay over the base of the earring post. Let the clay become bone dry before firing.

8. Fire the earrings at 1,470°F (800°C) for 30 minutes. The sterling silver backs won't melt at this lower temperature.

9. Wire brush the silver surface, then apply a blue-black liver-of-sulfur patina. Polish the earrings with a polishing cloth.

Plique-à-Jour

The French name of this traditional enameling technique means "membrane through which passes the light of day." The effect is reminiscent of a stained-glass window, non?

Tools & Materials

.1 ounce (2.8 g) medium- or quick-fire lump
    silver metal clay

⅜-inch (9.5 mm) star punch

Tissue blade

Coarse and fine emery boards

Transparent powdered enamel, any color

See-through film container

Glass or plastic rod

Distilled water

Clear-fire solution, available where jeweler's
    enameling supplies are sold

Sheet of mica, available where jeweler's
    enameling supplies are sold

Plastic spoon

Two-part epoxy

2 sterling silver earring posts with 2-mm pad

Tumbler with stainless steel shot

Instructions

1 Use mat-board spacers to roll out the metal clay to ¹⁄₁₆ inch (1.6 mm) thick. Using the star punch, cut a row of three stars for one earring, then repeat for the other earring.

2 Use the tissue blade to cut out a ½ x ¼-inch (9.5 mm x 3.2 cm) rectangle around the row of stars, leaving a space of ¼ inch (6 mm) at the top of the rectangle. This space will be needed later to attach the sterling silver earring post.

3 Let the clay dry to bone dry. File the edges with the coarse emery board, then the fine emery board. Fire the earrings, lying flat on a kiln shelf, at 1,650°F (900°C) for 10 minutes.

4 While the earrings are in the kiln, prepare the enamel. Transparent enamel must be washed or it will be cloudy. It's especially important to have clear and transparent enamel for this technique. Fill a see-through film container one-fourth full of transparent powdered enamel. Add tap water and stir vigorously with a glass or plastic rod; count to 10. Pour away the cloudy water until you get to the large grains of enamel at the bottom of the film container.

5 Repeat the washing process several times with plain tap water, until the standing water is clear. Pour off this water. Use distilled water for the final wash; it removes any of the minerals found in your local tap water.

6 Pour off the water and add three drops of clear-fire solution. Put the lid back on the film container to keep the enamel clean until you're ready to use it. Place the cooled (room-temperature) earrings on a sheet of mica. Scoop a small amount of enamel in the spoon. Use a paintbrush to push the wet enamel from the spoon into the star-shape openings. Using the enamel in this way is called "wet packing." Allow the water to evaporate, then add more enamel so it's flush with the top of the openings.

7 When the enamel is completely dry, place the mica on a kiln shelf and load it into the kiln, preheated to 1,500°F (816°C), for three minutes (this time is only a general guide because each color of enamel fuses at a different point). When the enamel is clear and glassy, remove your earrings from the kiln and allow them to cool.

8 Use the two-part epoxy to attach the sterling silver earring posts, centered in the top ¼ inch (6 mm) of the backs. The epoxy sets in five minutes and cures overnight.

9 Wire brush the earrings on a flat surface, then tumble them for 20 minutes to obtain a mirror finish.

CeCe's Cornucopias

These intricate earrings are rich with layered texture.

Tools & Materials

.5 ounce (5.6 g) slow-fire lump silver metal clay

Wooden craft stick

Craft knife

Coarse and fine emery boards

⅛-inch (3 mm) diameter bamboo skewer

Circle template, 1¾-inch (4.4 cm) diameter

Pin tool

Plastic beverage cap

Size #6 and #0 blender tools

Support material

Liver of sulfur

Polishing cloth

2 sterling silver eye pins

2 beads, each 4 mm in diameter

Flat-nose pliers

Round-nose pliers

2 sterling silver French ear wires

Instructions

1 Make a notched stamping tool. Cut off the rounded end of the wooden craft stick with the craft knife. Sand the cut end with the coarse emery board. Cut out a row of V-shape notches using a craft knife (see figure 1).

Figure 1

2 Make the mini-square stamping tool. Cut off the tapered end of the bamboo barbecue skewer with a craft knife. To create a square tip on the end, file two opposing sides of the bamboo skewer flat with a coarse emery board, then file the remaining two sides. Finish the edges with the coarse, then the fine, emery boards. Check that the tools create crisp impressions by stamping them into a piece of fresh clay.

3 With mat-board spacers, roll out the clay on a flexible work surface to ¹⁄₁₆ inch (1.6 mm) thick. Cut out a 1¾-inch diameter (4.4 cm) circle using a template and a pin tool. Roll the extra clay into a ball and mist it once, then wrap it tightly in plastic and put aside.

4 Roll the edge of a plastic beverage cap in a random pattern across the clay's surface.

5 Cut the circle in half. Mist one of the halves and cover it with plastic wrap.

6 Cut the half-circle into three pieces, as shown in figure 2.

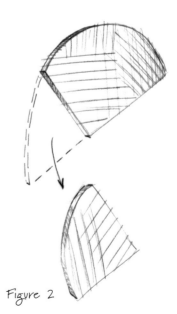

Figure 2

7 Slightly overlap the two interior cuts by ⅛ inch (3 mm), as shown in figure 3. Brush water on the overlaps to create secure seams.

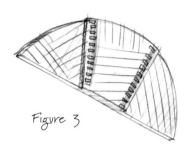

Figure 3

8 Stamp a pattern on top of the seams with the notched stamping tool.

9 Wrap the three-part seamed piece around the end of the #6 blender tool, as shown in figure 4. Let the clay overlap itself by ⅛ inch (3 mm) at the seam, and trim off the excess.

Figure 4

10 Close the cone. Wet the seam with water and overlap the edge by ⅛ inch (3 mm). Stamp a pattern on the seam with the notched stamping tool.

11 Roll clay into a small ball, brush it water, and place it one-third the way up from the bottom edge of the cone.

12 Stamp a square on top of the ball using the mini-square stamping tool.

13 Leave the clay cone on the end of the blender tool until it has dried to leather hard (stand the blender tool straight up in a cup).

14 Remove the cone from the blender tool. Blend the inside seam with the small (#0) blender tool.

15 Repeat steps 6 through 14 for the second earring.

16 Let the clay dry to bone dry before firing it. Fire the earrings upsidedown, with the tip of the cone submerged halfway in support material. Be careful not to get support material inside the cone, or the cone won't be able to shrink properly and the seams may break open.

17 Wire brush the earrings. Apply a patina of liver of sulfur until they're jet-black. Polish the earrings with a polishing cloth, leaving the black in the low textured areas.

18 Thread the sterling silver eye pin through the cone from the bottom. Add the bead.

19 With the flat-nose pliers, bend a 90° angle as close to the bead as possible. Cut off ¼ inch (6 mm) of the wire's tail.

20 Use the round-nose pliers to roll the tail toward the bend in the wire. It's important to clamp the pliers at the correct spot in order to obtain the best loop size.

21 Thread the ear wires onto the loops.

Puzzle Pieces

This wearable delight uses shining silver puzzle pieces to show off plenty of texture.

Instructions

1. Place the puzzle pieces or template (see figure 1) on a piece of clay, rolled out with matboard spacers to $\frac{1}{16}$ inch (1.6 mm) thick. Trace around them using the pin tool.

Figure 1

2. Use various seashells to stamp texture into the puzzle pieces.

3. Use the pin tool to poke holes in each of the protruding ends of the pieces.

4. Fire the bone-dry pieces flat on a kiln shelf at 1,650°F (900°C) for 10 minutes.

5. When the pieces have cooled, burnish them with the wire brush and soap and water. Dry them well.

6. Enhance the textures with magenta, red-violet, blue-purple, and steel-blue patinas. Directions for using a liver-of-sulphur patina are on page 44. Bring back the silver highlights by gently rubbing the surface with the polishing cloth.

Tools & Materials

.5 ounce (14 g) medium- or quick-fire lump silver metal clay

6 mini-puzzle pieces, or use the template in figure 1 at 100%

Seashells

Pin tool

Liver of sulphur

Polishing cloth

2 pairs of flat-nose pliers

7 sterling silver, 16-gauge jump rings, 4.4 mm in diameter

Sterling silver lobster clasp

7. Link the puzzle pieces together, using both pairs of flat-nose pliers to open and close the jump rings as shown in figure 2. Bending them open in this way keeps the rings from getting warped. Use a sterling jump ring to add the lobster clasp.

Figure 2

Charming Hearts

This extravagant array of textured
hearts makes a wonderful tinkling
sound on your wrist.

Instructions

1. Divide the lump of clay into six equal parts. With two different textures, one for each side, roll out each part to ⅟₁₆ inch (1.6 mm) thick. I used plastic texture sheets.

2. Move the clay to your work surface. Cut out six larger hearts.

3. Ball up the remaining clay, then divide it into nine equal parts. Again apply a pair of different textures to each side as you roll them out. Move the clay to the work surface and cut out eight smaller hearts.

4. While the clay is still moist, use a beverage stirrer to cut a hole in each of the hearts. Be careful not to cut too close to the edge.

5. When the clay is bone dry, file the edges with the coarse emery board. It's fine if all the hearts are slightly different shapes after this step; some variation is interesting. Finish the edges with the fine emery board.

6. Fire the hearts flat on a kiln shelf, close to each other but not touching, for 2 hours at 1,650°F (900°C).

7. Brush the hearts with a wire brush, then tumble them for 20 minutes. Apply liver-of-sulfur patina to the hearts to obtain a variety of magenta, red-violet, blue-purple, and steel blue colors. Use a polishing cloth to remove the patina from the high points.

Tools & Materials

1 ounce (28 g) slow-fire lump silver metal clay

Variety of textured surfaces

Two different-sized mini heart-shape cookie cutters

Beverage stirrer

Coarse and fine emery boards

Tumbler with stainless steel shot

Liver of sulphur

Polishing cloth

Wire cutters

14 pieces 18-gauge sterling silver wire, each 4 inches (10.2 cm) long

Flat-nose pliers

Round-nose pliers

Sterling silver linked bracelet

14 size 8° beads

8. To join the hearts to the bracelet links, make the Basic Jeweler's Wire Wrap, as described on page 46, adding a bead to each wrap before putting on the heart.

Flower Chain

Bright, shining
stones make this
bracelet come alive
with an updated
'60's style.

Instructions

The great thing about 950 silver eyelets is that you can fire them when you fire the main components, rather than separately. Only 950 silver can handle the highest firing temperature.

1 Make eight Groovy Flower Motifs by following steps 1–7 on page 53.

2 Roll out a marble-size ball of clay to the thickness of three playing cards.

3 Cut eight ½-inch (1.3 cm) squares, and press an eyelet at the top and bottom center edge of each one.

4 Use the stirrer to punch out a hole in the center of each square.

5 Brush the surface of the squares with water. Place a flower cutout on top of each square and press it lightly. Brush water around the edges of the flowers.

6 Fire the bone-dry piece flat on a kiln shelf at 1,650°F (900°C) for 10 minutes.

7 Wire brush the piece. For a sparkling mirror finish, tumble it with stainless steel shot for 25 minutes.

Tools & Materials

.5 ounce (14 g) medium-fire lump silver metal clay

8 pink sapphire cabochon laboratory-grown corundum, ³⁄₁₆-inch (5 mm) diameter

Playing cards

Flower-shape cutter, ⁷⁄₁₆ inch (1.1 cm)

Circle cutter, ³⁄₁₆ inch (5 mm)

Circle cutter, ½ inch (1.3 cm)

16 eyelets, 950 silver

Plastic beverage stirrer

Watercolor paintbrush

Tumbler with stainless steel shot

11 sterling silver 18-gauge jump rings, ⅛-inch (3 mm) diameter

2 pairs of flat-nose pliers

Sterling silver toggle clasp

8 Use a jump ring to link two squares together, back to back. Use flat-nose pliers in each hand to twist open the jump rings (see figure 2 on page 69). Continue until all the pieces are linked together.

9 Attach the clasp to the ends of the bracelet with jump rings.

Flowing River

*Silvery waves lap gently
at the edge of this
meditative piece.*

Instructions

1. For this project the clay must be rolled out a little thicker than typical. Roll out the metal clay, using craft sticks as spacers.

2. Use the tissue blade to cut a rectangle measuring 1½ x 2 inches (3.8 x 5 cm). Use the comb to make a graceful undulating pattern in the surface of the clay. Turn over the clay and repeat on the other side.

3. Trim the two long sides and one of the short sides with the tissue blade. Leave the textured edge of the last side as is.

4. Position the stirrer 1½ inches (3.8 cm) from the only textured edge and gently roll this edge over it. The overlap should be ½ inch (1.3 cm). Brush this seam with water and lightly press the clay surfaces together.

5. Make a mold with the button. Review the mold-making technique on pages 33–34.

6. Fill the mold with metal clay, then pop the clay from the mold while it's still moist. Brush an area with water and place the decorative clay button onto the moist clay. Lightly press them together.

7. Fire the bone-dry piece, flat on a kiln shelf, at 1,650°F (900°C) for two hours.

8. Wire brush the piece, then apply a blue-black liver-of-sulfur patina. Use the scrubbing pad to remove patina from the raised areas in the design. String the piece on leather cord.

Tools & Materials

.4 ounce (11.2 g) slow-fire metal clay

2 craft sticks

Tissue blade

Wide-tooth plastic comb

Plastic beverage stirrer

Decorative button, maximum ½-inch (1.3 cm) diameter

Mold-making materials

Liver of sulfur

Nylon scrubbing pad

Leather cord, 18 inches (45.7 cm) long

Spun Sugar

Sweet surprise! Delicate silver tracery floats over this medallion in a versatile display of surface embellishment.

Instructions

1. Cut a 1 x 1-inch (2.5 x 2.5 cm) square from metal clay rolled out with mat-board spacers to ¹⁄₁₆ inch (1.6 mm) thick. Round off the sharp corners by using the rounded corner of a playing card as a cutting template.

2. Make some thin slip by mixing water and metal clay to the consistency of thick cream. (See pages 26–27 for instructions.)

3. Load the slip into the syringe. Squirt it onto the square in a random pattern. This technique, borrowed from the ceramic world, is known as slip trailing. Extend the slip-trailed pattern beyond the edges of the clay surface. Allow the slip to dry.

4. Add another layer of slip and let it dry. Repeat the layering as often as you like for an interesting surface texture.

5. When the piece is bone dry, lift the square off the work surface and break away the excess slip. File the edges smooth with the coarse emery board.

6. Use your fingers to start a coil, then finish rolling it with the see-through ruler or plate glass, until it's ⅛ inch (3 mm) in diameter and 6 inches (15.2 cm) long. See photo 10 on page 28 for a demonstration of this technique.

7. Brush water around the outside edge of the square. Wrap the coil around the outer edge so it's touching the edge but not resting on top. Use the craft knife to cut through the coil where the ends overlap. Use the blender tool to blend the seam. Brush water on all the seams to ensure a secure connection.

Tools & Materials

.2 ounce (5.6 g) slow-fire lump silver metal clay

Craft knife

Playing card

Empty syringe

Coarse emery board

See-through ruler or sheet of plate glass with finished edges

Size #0 blender tool

Beverage stirrer

Liver of sulfur

Nylon scrubbing pad

8. To make the bail, roll out a pea-size ball of metal clay, and flatten it slightly. Poke a hole through the side with a stirrer. Let the bail dry to bone dry, then file it into a wedge shape.

9. Use thick slip to attach the bail to the square. Remove excess slip with the blender tool.

10. When the slip is completely dry the piece is ready to be fired. Fire it at 1,650°F (900°C), flat on a kiln shelf, for two hours.

11. Wire brush the piece, then apply a jet-black liver-of-sulfur patina. Rub the piece with the scrubbing pad to remove the patination from the topmost part of the surface.

Pin Dots

The smallest ripple in silver's smooth surface creates great texture, seen in the organic pattern of piercings in this pendant.

Instructions

1. Use a craft knife and ruler to cut a 1⅜ x 1⅜-inch (3.5 x 3.5 cm) square from a piece of metal clay rolled out with mat-baord spacers to ¹⁄₁₆-inch-thick (1.6 mm). Use the corner of a playing card to round off the square's corners.

2. Place the grid paper on top of the moist clay and use the pin tool to poke a hole all the way through the clay to the work surface at every intersection. Remove the grid paper. Let the clay dry until it's leather hard.

3. Lift the square and use the #6 blender tool to push into the pinholes, to create mini eruptions, like little volcanoes. Let the clay reach the bone-dry stage, face up on the work surface.

4. Roll out a coil of metal clay 6 inches (15.2 cm) long and ⅛ inch (3 mm) in diameter. Start it with your finger, then finish the rolling with the see-through ruler or plate glass.

5. Brush water around the outside edge of the square. Wrap the coil around the outer edge, making sure it's touching all the way around on the side edge but not on top.

6. Cut the coil where the ends overlap, then blend the seam with the #0 tool. Brush water on all the seams. Allow the clay to dry to bone dry.

7. To make the bail, roll out a clay slab, ¹⁄₁₆ inch thick (1.6 mm), that measures ¼ x 1 inch (6 mm x 2.5 cm).

Tools & Materials

.2 ounce (5.6 g) slow-fire lump silver metal clay

Craft knife

Ruler

Playing card

¼-inch (6 mm) grid paper

Pin tool

Size #6 and #0 blender tools

See-through ruler or sheet of plate glass with finished edges

Beverage stirrer

Craft stick

8. With the pendant piece lying face up, attach a short side of the bail to the underside of the pendant with a brush of water (see figure 1). Lay a beverage stirrer on top of the bail and fold over the bail, using a brush of water to attach it to the pendant.

Figure 1

9. Use the edge of the craft stick to press a ledge on the front edge of the bail, so that it makes a neatly finished edge.

10. Wait five minutes for the clay to slightly stiffen to the leather hard stage, then remove the stirrer. Allow the clay to dry to bone dry.

11. Fire the bone-dry pendant flat on the kiln shelf. This piece was simply wire brushed for a satin finish.

Sparkling Squares

Rows of dazzling
stones, set atop a
unique stamped
design, dot this
pendant.

Instructions

1. To make your own custom stamp, use a craft knife to cut a rectangle that measures ½ x ½ x ⅞ inch (1.3 x 1.3 x 2.2 cm) off the end of the eraser.

2. Referring to figure 1, cut eight V-shape notches as shown. These should be ¼ inch (6 mm) deep, down each of the sides.

Figure 1

3. Cut a small circle in the center of the stamp. Place the tip of the knife in the center; rotate it to make a ⅛ inch (3 mm) circle. Congratulations! You've just created your very own stamping tool.

4. Use mat-board spacers to roll out the clay to ¹⁄₁₆ inch (1.6 mm) thick.

5. Stamp nine impressions into the clay, using the same pressure each time. Cut a 2-inch (5 cm) square from the clay.

6. Punch a hole in the center of each stamped design with the beverage stirrer. Allow it to dry to bone dry.

Tools & Materials

.3 ounce (8.4 g) slow-fire lump silver metal clay

White plastic eraser

Craft knife

Beverage stirrer

Plastic beverage straw

Fine emery board

Thick slip

Size #6 or #0 blender tool

Clear acrylic ruler

Pencil

9 cubic zirconia stones, ⅛ inch (3 mm) diameter

Jeweler's tweezers

Liver of sulfur

Nylon scrubbing pad

7. To make the bail, roll out a strip of clay to ¹⁄₁₆ inch (1.6 mm) thickness. From it, cut a strip of clay ½ inch (1.3 cm) wide and 1½ inches (3.8 cm) long. Make a loop by folding it over a plastic drinking straw, as shown in figure 2.

8. Lightly brush water between the two layers of clay. Taper the end of the bail by flattening it with the rolling pin. Allow it to dry to bone dry.

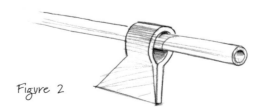

Figure 2

9 Refine the edges of the square with the emery board. Remove the straw and refine the edges of the bail with the emery board.

10 Apply thick slip at the tapered end of the front side of the bail. Attach the bail to the center back of the pendant. Use the blender tool to smooth away excess slip.

11 Place the piece right side up on a kiln shelf and let the slip dry for approximately 10 minutes.

12 The cubic zirconia stones will be held by ball settings. Roll out a coil ⅛ inch (3 mm) in diameter. Slice nine ⅛-inch (3 mm) pieces of the coil.

13 Roll a slice into a tiny ball. Tent the other eight pieces under plastic wrap so they don't dry out.

14 In the upper left corner, lightly brush the center of the stamped design with a little bit of water. Add the ball to the center of the hole.

15 Slightly flatten the ball with the clear acrylic ruler. Poke a conical hole in the center with the pencil, as shown in figure 3.

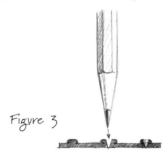

Figure 3

16 Set one of the stones in the hole with the jeweler's tweezers. Press the stone ⅛ inch (3 mm) below the surface. Set the eight remaining stones in the center of the stamped designs in the same way.

17 Fire the piece at 1,650°F (900°C) for 2 hours.

18 Wire brush the piece. Apply a steel-blue liver-of-sulfur patina, then rub it with the nylon scrubbing pad to give the silver a soft satin finish. The patina will stay in the low texture areas created by the stamp.

CeCe Wire. *Locket Box*, 2000.
1 x 1½ x ½ in (2.5 x 3.8 x 1.3 cm). PMC, and Nepalese chain.
PHOTO BY SANDRA STAMBAUGH

Water and Pebble

Nature's beauty can be
suggested with the
simplest design
elements, such as the
lines and spheres used
in this pendant.

Instructions

1. Texture the surface of a slab of clay, rolled with mat-board spacers to $\frac{1}{16}$ inch (1.6 mm) thick, using a plastic texture sheet, toothbrush, rubber stamp, or texturizing tool of your choice.

2. Use the craft knife and ruler to cut out a $1\frac{1}{2}$ x $2\frac{1}{4}$-inch (3.8 x 5.6 cm) rectangle, then round the corners, using the corner of a playing card as a template.

3. Roll out 11 coils of clay, each measuring $\frac{1}{8}$ inch (3 mm) in diameter and $2\frac{1}{4}$ inches (5.6 cm) long. Depending on your design, you may need a few more coils, or you might have extra pieces. As you make the coils, keep them under plastic wrap so they don't dry out.

4. Brush the face of the rectangle with water and place coils on the surface, allowing the ends to extend beyond the edges; let parts of the textured background show through. Remember to keep the coils under the plastic wrap until you're ready to use them so they don't crack.

5. When you've completed the design, use the craft knife to trim the coils flush with the edge of the rectangular backing.

Tools & Materials

.6 ounce (16.8 g) slow-fire
  metal clay

Plastic texture sheet, toothbrush,
  rubber stamp, or texturizing
  tool of your choice

Craft knife

Playing card

Watercolor paintbrush

Coarse emery board

See-through ruler

Size #0 blender tool

Tumbler with stainless steel shot

Liver of sulfur

6. Make an assortment of little clay balls in different sizes. Place the balls into your design with a brush of water. Let the piece reach the bone-dry stage, then refine the edges with the emery board.

7. Roll out a coil of clay measuring $\frac{1}{8}$ inch (3mm) in diameter and 8 inches (20.3 cm) long. Use your fingers at first, then use the see-through ruler to finish it, so it has a uniform diameter from end to end.

8 Brush water around the outside edge of the rectangle. Wrap the coil around the outer edge so it touches the sides but not the top. Cut the coil where the ends overlap (see figure 1). Blend the seam. Brush water on all the seams.

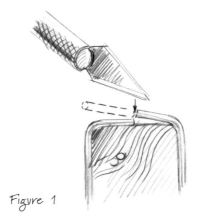

Figure 1

9 To make the bail, cut a coil measuring ⅛ inch (3 mm) in diameter and 1½ inches (3.8 cm) long. Shape the bail and attach it to the rec-

tangle, as shown in figure 2. Brush water along the seam. Add a ball to each end of the bail. Let the piece become bone dry.

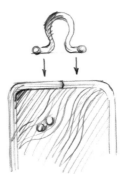

Figure 2

10 Fire the pendant, lying directly on the kiln shelf, for two hours at 1,650°F (900°C).

11 Finish the piece with a wire-brush finish. Tumble in stainless steel shot for 40 minutes, then apply the liver-of-sulfur patina for a rainbow of colors in the magenta, red-violet, and blue-purple range.

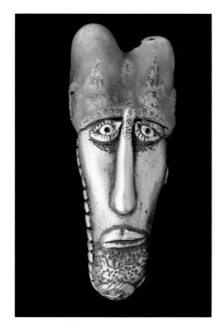
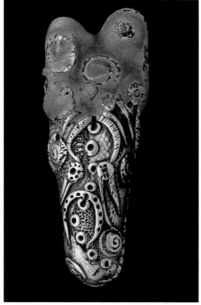

Carl Stanley. *King Midas* (front and back), 2002. Bead: 3 x 1¾ x 1 in. (7.6 x 4.4 x 2.5 cm). Silver clay; frosted enamel, acid patina and brush finished. PHOTO BY PATRICK FLANNERY.

Rippling Sands

Starting with a single, simple shape, this carved design grew in a way that reminds me of restless desert winds.

Instructions

You might want to try the Ashanti earrings on page 57 before tackling this project. Until you're comfortable with the carving technique, keep the design simple; remember that curved lines are harder to control than straight lines.

1 Use mat-board spacers to roll out metal clay to ¹⁄₁₆ inch (1.6 mm) thick.

2 Using the craft knife and ruler, cut a 1¾ x 1¾-inch (4.4 x 4.4 cm) square; angle off the corners. Allow the clay to dry to bone dry.

3 Draw the design you wish to carve on the surface. The pencil lead will burn away later.

4 Use the pin tool to scribe into the pencil lines. Doing so creates a shallow trench that will make the carving easier.

5 Hold the carving tool at a 22° angle, and carve away only a small amount of material (see figure 1).

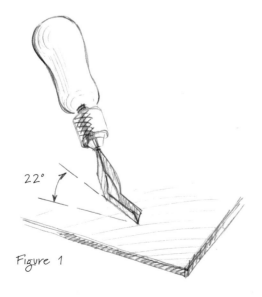

22°

Figure 1

Tools & Materials

.4 ounce (11.2 g) slow-fire lump silver metal clay

Craft knife

Ruler

Pin tool

Linoleum carving tool and #1 tip

Coarse emery board

See-through ruler or sheet of plate glass with finished edges

Size #0 blender tool

Beverage stirrer

Alumina hydrate

Tumbler with stainless steel shot

Fine-point permanent marker

6 Increase the angle of the tool to 45° and go over the design again.

7 Use the coarse emery board and file the edges. At the corners, file round the blunt edges.

8 Roll out a coil of metal clay 8 inches (20.3 cm) long and ⅛ inch (3 mm) in diameter. Use the ruler or glass to help you make it even.

9 Brush water around the outside edge of the square. Wrap the coil around the outer edge, positioning the seam at the top center of the pendant. Later, when you add the bail, the seam will be hidden. Be sure the coil touches the sides, but not the top of the clay, all the way around the pendant. Cut the coil where the ends overlap. Blend the seam. To assure a good connection, brush water wherever the pieces touch each other.

10 For the bail, roll out a pea-size ball of metal clay, then gently shape it into an egg shape. Press down on the egg to flatten it slightly. Punch a hole through the wide end with a beverage stirrer.

11 Brush some water at the top center of the pendant and position the bail. Press lightly to ensure a good bond.

12 Once the pendant is bone dry, place on a kiln shelf. Support the bail with some alumina hydrate (see figure 2). Fire the piece for two hours at 1,650°F (900°C).

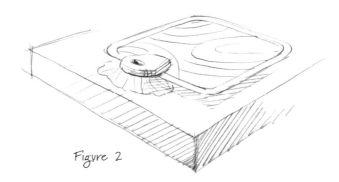

Figure 2

13 Wire brush the piece, then tumble it for 40 minutes. To create a high-contrast finish, darken the crevices with a fine-point permanent marker.

Candice Wakumoto. *Papa La'au x 7,* 2002. 9 x 9⅝ x ⅝ in. (22.9 x 24.5 x 1.6 cm). Hand-formed and carved silver metal clay; 22k, 18k, citrine, freshwater pearls, sterling silver; solder construction, handset gem stones. Collection of Alice Korach. PHOTO BY LARRY SANDERS.

Folk Art Heart

The shape of this dimpled heart pays homage to a simple folk-art style and its golden accent brings the design to a gleaming focal point.

Instructions

1. Make a template by drawing a heart shape onto card stock that is 2½ inches (6.4 cm) long. Cut out the shape.

2. Using mat-board spacers, roll out the slow-fire metal clay to ¹⁄₁₆ inch (1.6 mm) thick.

3. Use the pin tool and template to cut out the heart shape from the clay.

4. Texture the surface with the ballpoint. Let the clay become bone dry.

5. To make the bail, roll out a pea-size ball of metal clay to ¹⁄₁₆ inch (1.6 mm) thick, and cut a ¼ x 1-inch (6 mm x 2.5 cm) strip from it.

6. Fold the strip of clay over the straw and moisten it where the two ends touch each other. Allow it to dry to leather hard.

7. Attach the bail to the back of the heart with some metal clay slip, as shown in figure 1.

Figure 1

Tools & Materials

.4 ounce (11.2 g) slow-fire lump silver metal clay

.0625 ounce (1.8 g) gold metal clay [this amount of clay is equal to one-fourth of a standard ¼-ounce (7 g) package]

.1 ounce (2.8 g) medium-fire lump silver metal clay

Card stock

Pin tool

Ballpoint

Craft knife

Plastic drinking straw

Beverage stirrer

Tumbler with stainless steel shot

8. Before you open the package of gold, carefully wash your tools, work surface, and hands. You don't want to mix small particles of silver clay in with the gold. For this piece I used ¹⁄₁₆ of an ounce of gold metal clay (a quarter of the package). Make a pea-size ball of gold metal clay.

9. Flatten the ball slightly and poke a hole through it with the beverage stirrer. Save the hole—this is gold!

10. Allow the gold piece to dry to bone dry. Fire the gold piece flat on a kiln shelf at 1,830°F (1,000°C) for two hours. Don't finish the surface.

11 Fire the silver heart flat on a kiln shelf at 1,650°F (900°C) for two hours. Don't finish the surface on this piece either. The unfinished surface is porous, and this open surface is necessary for joining the pieces.

12 To attach the gold ornament to the silver heart, center a pea-size ball of medium-fire metal clay in the upper part of the silver heart. Press the gold ornament onto the clay ball. The clay must come up through the hole, as shown in figure 2. If it doesn't, take the two pieces apart, remove the clay, and reshape the ball with more clay. Use the end of a brush to flatten the top of the clay into a rivet.

13 Fire the clay at 1,650°F (900°C) for 2 hours. The longer firing time ensures the strongest bond between the slow- and medium-fire clays and reduces the risk of losing the gold ornament later.

14 Wire brush the surface, then tumble the piece for 40 minutes to a beautiful mirror finish.

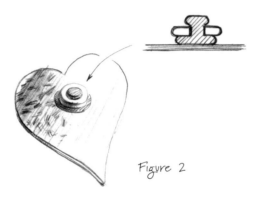

Figure 2

Susan Amendolara. *New Growth II,* 1998.
4 x 1½ x ¼ in. (10.2 x 3.8 cm x 6 mm).
Silver metal clay flower; cast sterling silver,
24k gold foil applied in the kem boo technique.
PHOTO BY ARTIST.

Moon in the Sky

The colorful fire caught in this pendant comes from a dazzling dichroic glass cabochon. A golden sapphire set among highly polished silver balls adds even more excitement to this fancy design.

Instructions

Using glass in combination with metal clay is an exciting way to add brilliant color to your pieces. I learned about using dichroic glass from the metal clay master, Mary Ann Devos.

1 Use mat-board spacers to roll out medium-fire lump clay to ¹⁄₁₆ inch (1.6 mm) thick. Place the glass cabochon on the surface of the clay.

2 For the bezel, make a coil of metal clay that is one-half to three-quarters of the height of the cabochon and long enough to loosely wrap around it. Taper one end.

3 Wrap the coil around the dichroic glass cabochon, overlapping the seam, and cut away the excess (see figure 1). With your finger, lightly press down on the coil all the way around the glass cabochon. Further secure the seams by brushing water on them. This ensures that the glass won't seep out during the firing where the bezel joins the back piece during the firing.

Tools & Materials

.7 ounce (19.6 g) medium-fire lump silver metal clay

Dichroic glass cabochon, ³⁄₄ inch (1.9 cm) diameter

Craft knife

Plastic drinking straw

Size #6 or #0 blender tool

Golden sapphire cabochon laboratory-grown corundum, 4 mm diameter

Beverage stirrer

Tumbler with stainless steel shot

Sterling silver ball chain, 16 inches (40.6 cm) long

4 Cut the background of the pendant, using a card-stock photocopy at 100%, of the template shown in figure 2.

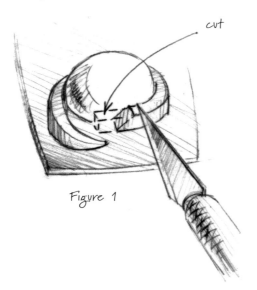

cut

Figure 1

Figure 2

5   To create a bail, bring the top edge of the rectangle over a plastic straw to within ¼ inch (6 mm) from the bezel setting. Brush water along the seam to assure secure adhesion.

6   Decorate the pendant with small balls of metal clay in a variety of sizes. Remember to brush water on the clay before adding each ball.

7   While the balls are still moist, push dimples into some of the larger balls with the end of the blender tool. Notice I added a dimpled ball to the bail, too, which helps to visually incorporate it into the design.

8   Set the sapphire with a ball setting, as described on page 38.

9   After the piece is bone dry, carefully remove the straw. Fire the piece on a kiln shelf to 1,470°F (800°C) for 25 to 30 minutes. When the firing is complete, open the door to crash-cool the piece. When the pyrometer reads 1,000°F (538°C) quickly shut the kiln door. This prevents devitrification, or clouding of the glass. Allow the piece to cool to room temperature before opening the kiln door again (if the glass cools too quickly at this stage, it could crack).

10 Wire brush the piece. Tumble it for 20 minutes with stainless steel shot. The shot won't scratch the glass. Thread the piece onto the ball chain.

Barbara Becker Simon. *Untitled,* 2000. Largest: 1 x ¾ x ¾ in. (2.5 x 1.9 x 1.9 cm). Hollow lamp worked glass around metal clay "spool." PHOTO BY LARRY SANDERS.

Double Happiness

This sleekly modern pendant uses a Japanese kanji that means "double happiness."

Instructions

You can find a canapé cutter shaped like a calligraphic character in most Asian grocery stores.

1 Use mat-board spacers to roll out the silver clay to ¹⁄₁₆ inch (1.6 mm) thick. Using an old toothbrush, texture the surface of the moist clay.

2 Use the tissue blade to cut a 2 x 1½-inch (5 x 3.8 cm) rectangle from the rolled-out clay. Allow it to dry to leather hard.

3 Roll out more silver clay to ⅛ inch (3 mm) thick on a clear plastic report sleeve. Cut out the double happiness symbol. Allow the piece to dry to leather hard so you can more easily remove the *kanji's* intricate design from the plastic without damaging it.

4 Moisten the surface of the clay rectangle with water. Place the *kanji* on top.

5 With your finger, firmly press down on the *kanji*. To ensure a strong seam, brush water around the edges of the design. Set the piece aside to dry to bone dry.

6 To make the hanging device, use your fingers to roll some metal clay into a thick log, ¼ inch (6 mm) diameter and 3 inches (7.6 cm) long. Use the craft-stick spacers to roll a ³⁄₁₆-inch-thick (5 mm) slab of metal clay.

Tools & Materials

.4 ounce (11.2 g) slow-fire lump silver metal clay

Toothbrush

Tissue blade

Clear plastic report sleeve

Double happiness canapé cutter

Watercolor paintbrush

2 pairs craft sticks, glued together to make 2 spacers

Size #0 blender tool

Plastic pallet knife

Alumina hydrate

Liver of sulfur

Polishing cloth

7 Referring to figure 1, use the tissue blade to cut a square rod, ³⁄₁₆ x ³⁄₁₆ inch (5 x 5 mm); it should be at least 3 inches (7.6 cm) long.

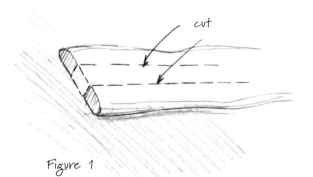

Figure 1

8 Let the rod dry, then cut a 1½-inch-section (3.8 cm) from it.

9 Cut two ½-inch (1.3 cm) pieces. On one end of each short piece carve a groove, ⅛ inch (3 mm) deep, as shown in figure 2.

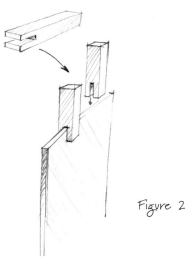

Figure 2

10 Add some slip into each groove, then slide them onto the top of the pendant (see figure 2). Use the blender tool to remove excess slip from around the seam. Allow the piece to dry.

11 Holding the piece upright, use the palette knife to apply a generous dollop of thick slip to the ends of the upright pieces. Attach the crosspiece to the uprights.

12 Lay the piece flat. Attach small clay balls with water where the crosspiece joins the uprights. With the end of a paintbrush, press dimples into the balls.

13 Fire the pendant for two hours on a kiln shelf dusted with a ⅛-inch (3 mm) bed of alumina hydrate. The alumina helps all the parts to shrink at an equal rate.

14 Use the wire brush with soap and water to give the piece a satin finish. Color the pendant blue-gray in a solution of liver of sulfur. Remove the patina with the polishing cloth so the double happiness symbol stands out from the background.

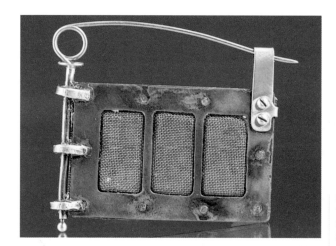

Chris Darway. *From the 1½ x 1 Series,* 1999. 1½ x 1 x ⅛ in. (3.8 x 2.5 cm x 3 mm). Silver metal clay; titanium, sterling silver, 14k gold, stainless steel. PHOTO BY CHET BOLINS.

Serpentine

*A single gleaming coil
creates a subtle serpent
motif for your finger.*

Instructions

Sizing a ring seems a little tricky at first, but it's really quite simple. Measure the knuckle of the appropriate finger, then add 12 percent (for shrinkage) to this measurement. Remember the old carpenter's adage: Measure twice, cut once.

1 Cut a ½ x 6-inch (1.3 x 15.2 cm) strip of paper. Wrap the paper around the knuckle of your finger. Make a pencil mark where the paper overlaps, and mark an arrow to the inside of your line.

2 Use the shrinkage ruler (or do the math) to add 12 percent to the length of the paper strip, and mark the new length on it.

3 Wrap electrical tape around an end of the PVC pipe until its circumference matches that of the paper pattern. You will build your ring on this form, or mandrel.

4 Roll a marble-size piece of clay into an irregular coil that is two times longer than your paper pattern, making some areas thicker than others. Taper one end of the coil for the tail and round the head end.

5 Wrap the coil around the mandrel, as shown in figure 1. Make sure the head and tail touch the body.

Figure 1

Tools & Materials

.1 ounce (2.8 g) medium- or quick-fire lump silver metal clay

Metal clay shrinkage ruler

Electrical tape

Piece of PVC pipe, ¼ inch (6 mm) diameter

Alumina hydrate

Tumbler with stainless steel shot

6 Brush water on the entire surface of the ring and allow it to dry to leather hard.

7 Carefully slide the ring off the electrical tape, set it on its side, and let it dry to bone dry.

8 Fire the ring flat in a bed of alumina hydrate ¹⁄₁₆ inch (1.6 mm) thick. Read page 22 to learn about the safety concerns of alumina hydrate.

9 Use the wire brush with soap and water to get a satin finish. Tumble the piece for 25 minutes.

Flower Power

Illuminated by its pale pink stone, this hippie-era flower-motif ring sparkles with a gently nostalgic light.

Instructions

1 Make one Groovy Flower Motif, as described in steps 1–7 on page 53, for the top of the ring.

2 Determine your ring size. Cut a ⅜ x 6-inch (9.5 mm x 15.2 cm) strip of paper. Wrap the paper around the knuckle of the ring finger, marking the place where the paper overlaps. Lay the paper out flat and mark an arrow to the inside of the line.

3 Use the shrinkage ruler to add 12 percent to the length. Subtract ⅛ inch (3 mm) from this measurement. Mark, then cut, the paper strip to the new length.

4 Roll out some metal clay to 1/16 inch (1.6 mm) thick. Use the paper pattern as a template to cut a clay strip.

5 Use the credit card to press parallel lines lengthwise into the surface of the moist clay.

6 Fire the bone-dry band and flower motif, both lying flat, on a kiln shelf for 10 minutes at 1,650°F (900°C).

7 When the band has cooled, bend it into a ring shape. With your thumbs together, start bending each end of the band around the handle of the pin tool, using it as a mandrel. Do this slowly, working at opposite ends of the band a little at a time. If you work too quickly, the band could break. Don't bend the band into a complete circle; allow a ⅛-inch (3 mm) opening.

Tools & Materials

.1 ounce (2.8 g) medium-fire lump silver metal clay

Playing cards

Flower-shape cutter, 7/16 inch (1.1 cm)

Circle cutter, 3/16 inch (5 mm)

Circle cutter, ½ inch (1.3 cm)

Plastic beverage stirrer, less than 3/16-inch (5mm) diameter

1 pink sapphire cabochon laboratory-grown corundum, 3/16 inch (5 mm) diameter

Metal clay shrinkage ruler

Craft knife

Credit card

Pin tool

Size #0 blender tool

Alumina hydrate

Tumbler with stainless steel shot

8 Roll a pea-size piece of clay out to a coil 3/16 inches (5 mm) thick. Cut the coil into two ½-inch (1.3 cm) pieces. Press the coils onto the ends of the band, as shown in figure 1.

Figure 1

9 Press the flower motif onto the moist coils of fresh silver clay. Most of the clay should spread under the flower motif. With the blending tool, blend the clay between the two parts of the ring, as shown in figure 2.

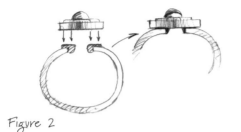

Figure 2

10 Allow the new clay to dry completely. Fire the ring, flower side down, in a shallow bed of alumina hydrate, ⅛ inch (3 mm) deep, for 2 hours at 1,650°F (900°C), to achieve maximum strength.

11 Treat the ring to a wire-brush finish. For a final mirror finish, put the ring in a tumbler with stainless steel shot for 25 minutes.

Nancy Karpel. *Mayan Cenote - Fertility Pendant,* 2000. 2⅝ x 1⅝ x 3/16 in. (6.6 x 4.1 cm x 5 mm). Silver metal clay, gold metal clay; enamel, sapphire, 18k gold, 14k gold, boulder opal, epidote in quartz, sterling silver, fine silver, 22k gold leaf. PHOTO BY FRANK POOLE.

Celie Fago. *Untitled,* 2001. Size 7½ x ½ in. (19 x 1.3 cm) width. Silver metal clay with gold metal clay accents, satin finish. PHOTO BY ROBERT DIAMANTE.

Deco Design

The precision of these art deco–inspired pyramids creates a strong relief pattern against the ribbed band.

Instructions

This geometric texture is made from something you may already have in the kitchen: a meat tenderizer!

1 To make the top of the ring, first make a silicone mold (see pages 33–34 for information on mold material). Push the highly textured end of the meat tenderizer into the mold material, supporting the handle with a stack of books or something similar so it's level. Remove the tenderizer when the mold compound has cured (in 5 to 30 minutes, depending on which type you use).

2 Roll a nickel-size ball from very moist slow-fire clay (a fresh package) onto the work surface. Taper one end so the ball becomes an egg shape. Push the smaller end of the clay into the center of the mold, as shown in photos 21 and 22 on page 33. Leave the clay in the mold for 10 minutes or more, until it becomes leather hard.

3 Carefully remove the metal clay from the mold. Silicone mold compound is somewhat oily and very flexible, so it should be easy to release the silver clay from it.

4 Select the best part of the pattern and use the tissue blade to cut out a square that measures four pyramid rows on each side.

5 Once it's bone dry, use a coarse emery board to file the edges and round off the sharp corners of the piece.

Tools & Materials

.3 ounce (8.4 g) slow-fire lump silver metal clay

.1 ounce (2.8 g) medium-fire lump silver metal clay

Two-part silicone mold compound

Meat tenderizer

Books or other weight

Tissue blade

Coarse emery board

See-through ruler or 4 x 8 x ¼-inch (10.2 x 20.3 cm x 6 mm) piece of plate glass

Craft knife

Size #0 blender tool

Metal clay shrinkage ruler

Card stock

Pin tool

Alumina hydrate

Tumbler with stainless steel shot

6 Roll out a coil of moist slow-fire metal clay, 5 inches (12.7 cm) long and ⅛ inch (3 mm) wide. Start by rolling with your finger, then use the see-through ruler or the glass to finish it (refer to photo 10 on page 28).

7 Brush water around the outside edge of the square and wrap the coil around the outer edge. Be certain the coil touches all of the square's edge but not its top. Cut the coil where the ends overlap.

8 Use the #0 blender tool to blend the seam, then wet the seams with a brush moistened with water.

9 Let the piece dry to bone dry, then fire it at 1,650°F (900°C), flat on a kiln shelf, for two hours.

10 While the ring cap is firing, make the ring band.

11 Determine your ring size. Cut a ½ x 6-inch (1.3 x 15.2 cm) strip of paper. Wrap it around the knuckle of the ring finger, marking the place where the strip overlaps. Lay the paper out flat and mark an arrow at the side of the line.

12 Use the shrinkage ruler to add 12 percent to the length. Subtract ⅜ inch (9.5 mm) from this number.

13 Photocopy the ring band template (see figure 1) onto card stock Adjust the card template's length to the length of the paper strip, adding or subtracting length as needed at the narrower middle part of the template.

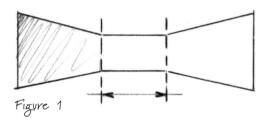

Figure 1

14 Use the mat-board spacers to roll out the medium-fire metal clay to ¹⁄₁₆ inch (1.6 mm) thick.

15 Lay the band template onto the clay and cut around it. Press the edge of the ruler into the surface of the moist clay to make a linear pattern. Leave the back of the band plain.

16 Fire the bone-dry band flat on a kiln shelf at 1,650°F (900° C) for 10 minutes.

17 When the band has cooled, bend it into a ring shape. With your thumbs together, start bending first one end of the band around the handle of the pin tool, using it as a mandrel, then the other. Do this slowly, alternating beween the opposite ends, a little at a time. If you do it too quickly, the band could break. Stop bending when the ends are ⅜ inch (9.5 mm) apart. Check to see if this will fit your finger; you can make adjustments at this time.

18 Roll out a coil of medium-fire metal clay ³⁄₁₆ inch (5 mm) thick and 2 inches (5 cm) long. Cut the coil into two ⅝-inch (1.6 cm) pieces.

19 Place the ring top face down on the work surface. Brush the back with water. Position the coils on the back so they line up with ends of the band. Press the band's ends into the coils (see figure 2 on page 102). The coils create a mechanical hold, a practical design to keep the ring together.

20 Allow the new clay to dry completely. Refire the ring at 1,650°F (900°C) for two hours with the ring cap face down in a ⅛ inch (3 mm) bed of alumina hydrate.

21 To finish the ring, use the wire brush with soap and water, then tumble it for 25 minutes.

Sun-Ra

A glittering offering to the Egyptian sun god. Gleaming gold inlay marries beautifully with the silver band in this elegant unisex design.

Instructions

You'll need a ceramic ring plug for this project. Ring plugs are only available in whole numbers; round a half-size measurement to the next larger whole size.

1 Use mat-board spacers to roll out the silver metal clay to ¹⁄₁₆ inch (1.6 mm) thick.

2 Wrap a strip of paper around the larger end of the ring plug. Cut a strip of clay ⁷⁄₁₆ inches (1.1 cm) wide and equal to the length of the paper strip.

3 Wrap the top (the larger end) of the ring plug with masking tape so the sticky side faces out.

4 Taper one end of the ring band with the rolling pin. Starting with the larger end, wrap the clay around the taped end of the plug. The masking tape holds it in place.

5 Overlap the seam and cut the clay where the taper ends (see figure 1). Brush some water on the seam, and use the blender tool to blend the clay to create an invisible seam. Let the band dry to leather hard.

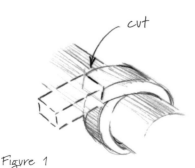

Figure 1

Tools & Materials

.1 ounce (2.8 g) slow-fire lump silver metal clay

.0625 ounce (1.75 g) gold metal clay

High-fire ceramic ring plug, for the ring size you need (available where metal clay supplies are sold)

Masking tape

Tissue blade

Rolling pin

Craft knife

Watercolor paintbrush

Size #0 blender tool

Plastic beverage straw

See-through ruler or sheet of plate glass with finished edges

Airtight container

Ceramic tape (purchase where metal clay supplies are sold)

Transparent tape

Alumina hydrate

Tumbler with stainless steel shot

6 Use mat-board spacers to roll out a marble-size ball of clay to ¹⁄₁₆ inch (1.3 mm) thick. Use the plastic beverage straw to cut an even number of equally spaced circles in a row. This ring, a size 7, has 12 holes. Cut a band of clay, ⁵⁄₁₆ inches (8 mm) wide and long enough to wrap around the first ring band you made, so the circles run down the center. Use the rolling pin to taper one end.

7 Brush water around the solid band and lay the circle-cut band on top of it. Lightly press down on the cut band. Overlap the seam and cut the clay where the taper ends, as you did in step 5.

8 Blend the seam. Don't be concerned about altering the circle pattern—just focus on making a well-crafted seam. Trim both sides of the band with the tissue blade and set it aside for 2 to 3 minutes to stiffen it slightly.

9 With the straw, recut the circle at the seam, cutting only through the first layer of clay and not into the leather-hard band underneath it. If the circle doesn't come out cleanly, lift it out with the pin tool. Let the clay dry to bone dry.

10 Now is the time to work with the gold metal clay. Before you open the package, carefully wash your tools, work surface, and hands. You don't want to mix small particles of silver clay with the gold.

11 Use the see-through ruler or plate glass to roll out a coil of gold clay ⅛ inch (3 mm) thick and 1 inch (2.5 cm) long. Cut ⅛-inch-thick (3 mm) crosswise slices from it (cut half the number of circles in the top band).

12 Wrap the remaining gold clay tightly, seal it with transparent tape, and place in an airtight container. Mist the gold clay circles with water and tent them under plastic wrap. Roll one slice into a ball.

13 Start with the circle at the seam. Brush some water into the bottom and sides of the opening. Put the ball of gold into it and press the clay lightly with your finger. Finish by pressing down the gold firmly with the see-through ruler, until it's just higher than the surface of the silver band. Fill every other hole. Allow the piece to dry to bone dry.

14 Slide the ring off the ring plug and remove the masking tape.

15 Wrap the bottom of the ring plug with ceramic tape and attach it to the plug with transparent tape. Place the ring on the ceramic tape (see figure 2). Stand the ring plug in a shallow bed of alumina hydrate and fire the clay for 2 hours at 1,650°F (900°C).

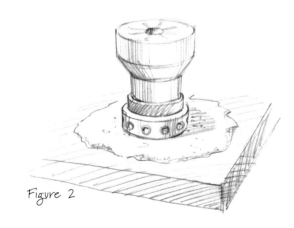

Figure 2

16 Wire brush the ring, then tumble it for 20 minutes to achieve a mirror finish. The gold will shine against the silver.

Teddy Bear

Get a younger artist to help you create and finish this bear pin with simple tools that used to belong in the kitchen. For practice, make a batch of teddy bear cookies first.

Tools & Materials

.2 ounce (5.6 g) medium-fire metal clay

Playing cards

Teddy-bear-shape cookie cutter, 1½ inches
  tall (3.8 cm), or figure 1 template at 100%

Heart-shape pattern cutter, ³⁄₁₆ inch
  (5 mm)

Jeweler's tweezers, 6 inches (15.2 cm)
  or longer

Stainless steel mixing bowl

Stainless steel spoon

Two-part epoxy

Nickel tie-tac post and clutch

Figure 1

Instructions

1 Roll out the metal clay to the thickness of three playing cards.

2 Use the cookie cutter to cut out the bear (or use figure 1 as a template).

3 Use the heart-shape pattern cutter to cut out a heart. Allow the bear to dry to bone dry.

4 Lay the piece flat on a kiln shelf and fire it at 1,650°F (900°C) for 10 minutes.

5 After the kiln temperature drops to 400°F (204°C), use tweezers to move the bear from the kiln into the mixing bowl filled with water.

6 Burnish the surface of the teddy bear by rubbing the convex part of the stainless spoon in a circular motion. This gives Mr. Bear a mirror finish.

7 Mix the two-part epoxy according to the package directions. Attach the nickel tie-tac post on the back of the bear just below the heart.

8 Set aside to dry overnight. In the morning, the pin is ready to wear or to give as a gift.

The Natural

Make a brooch
that features the
captivating, natural
qualities of torn clay
and a seashell
texture.

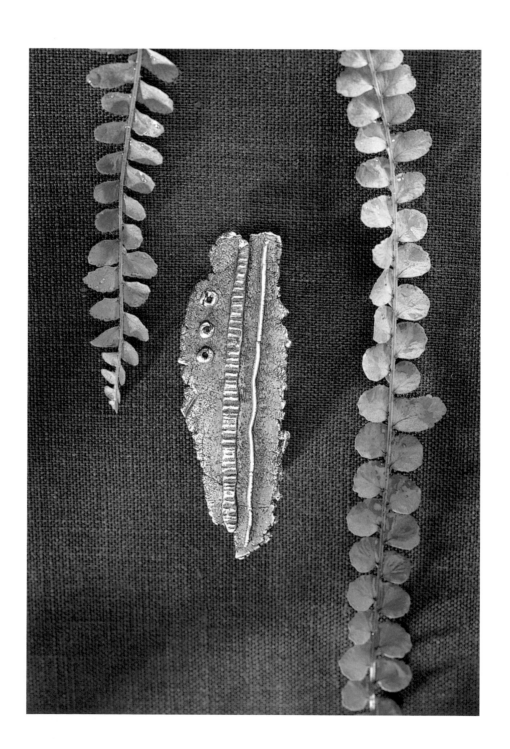

Tools & Materials

.2 ounce (5.6 g) slow-fire lump silver metal clay

Syringe quick-fire silver metal clay

Toothbrush

Craft knife

Seashell

Three-part pin set [sterling silver pin catch, joint, and 1½-inch-long (3.8 cm) nickel pin stem]

Wire brush

Liver of sulfur

Nylon scrubbing pad

Instructions

1 Use mat-board spacers to roll out a rectangle of metal clay ¹⁄₁₆ inch (1.6 mm) thick. The finished size of this piece is 3¼ x 1 inch (8.2 x 2.5 cm), so start with a rectangle that is slightly larger.

2 Texture the surface with a toothbrush. With your thumbs close together, create an interesting edge by tearing the clay (see photo 9 on page 28). If you don't care for the torn shape that results, roll the clay into a ball and start over.

3 Roll out a coil of clay with your fingers that is ⅛ inch (3 mm) in diameter and 4 inches (10.2 cm) in length.

4 Use the craft knife to slice three ⅛-inch (3mm) pieces from the coil and set them aside.

5 Brush water on the surface of the torn clay, then add the coil to the moist surface. Press it lightly with your finger. Tear away the extra clay that extends over each end.

6 Press a seashell texture into the clay, flattening the coil as you go.

7 Roll the three pieces you cut in step 4 into small balls.

8 Brush the surface of the clay with water and place the balls on the moist surface. Create a hole in the center of each ball by pushing the end of the paintbrush into it.

9 Use your fingers to make a coil of clay that is ¹⁄₁₆ inch (1.6 mm) in diameter and 4 inches (10.2 cm) in length.

10 Brush water on the surface of the torn clay and place the coil on the moist surface. Press it lightly with your finger to attach it. Tear away the extra clay.

11 Fire the bone-dry piece flat on a kiln shelf for 2 hours at 1,650°F (900°C).

12 Attach the pin back, as described on pages 46–47.

13 Wire brush the silver. Develop a liver-of-sulfur patina in a range of violet, blue-purple, and steel blue colors. Use the nylon scrubbing pad to remove patina from the raised areas in the design.

Alphabet Soup

This bold design employs tiny pasta letters and rubber stamps to create two different but complementary textures.

Tools & Materials

.8 ounce (22.4 g) medium- or quick-fire
   lump silver metal clay

Syringe medium-fire silver metal clay

Playing cards

Alphabet rubber stamps, ⅜ inch (9.5 mm)

Square lid of a container of lump
   metal clay

Ruler

¼-inch-high (6 mm) pasta letters (some
   brands include numbers)

Coarse and fine emery boards

Three-part sterling silver pin set [pin catch,
   joint, and 1-inch-long (2.5-cm) nickel pin
   stem]

Liver of sulfur

Instructions

1 Roll out the metal clay to the thickness of
three playing cards.

2 Rubber-stamp letters randomly onto the surface of the clay to create an overall surface
texture. Stamp the letters upside down, side-
ways, angled, and overlapped to create an
interesting random pattern.

3 Using the lid of a metal clay container like a
cookie cutter, cut out a 1⅞-inch (4.7 cm)
square with rounded corners. The clear plastic lid makes it easy to zero in on your
favorite stamped area.

4 Make the remaining clay into a ball and,
again, roll it out to the thickness of three
playing cards. Cut out a 1⅜-inch (3.5 cm)
square.

5 Sprinkle the surface with alphabet pasta,
pressing them lightly into the surface of the
moist clay.

6 Moisten the surface of the stamped piece
with water. Place the pasta piece on top of it.
This leaves a ¼-inch (6 mm) border showing.

7 Once the piece is bone dry, file the edges
smooth with the emery boards.

8 Fire the piece flat on a kiln shelf at 1,650°F
(900°C) for 10 minutes. Let it cool.

9 Attach the sterling silver pin catch and joint
and fire the piece, as described on pages
46–47.

10 Wire brush the surface, then use the tumbler
to burnish the piece to a mirror finish. Use
the liver of sulfur to develop a blue-black
patina. Finish by rubbing the surface with a
polishing cloth.

African Mask

Inspired by the carved wooden masks of South Africa, this vigorous high-relief design was made using slabs, balls, and coils. Multi-layered finishing techniques make the most of the various textures.

Instructions

1 Use mat-board spacers to roll out the metal clay to ¹⁄₁₆ inch (1.6 mm) thick. Lay the circle template on the clay and cut around it with the pin tool. Texture the surface with the toothbrush.

2 For the facial features, roll out a coil of clay approximately ⅛-inch (3 mm) in diameter and 2 inches (5 cm) long. Cut the coil into six pieces, each ⅛ inch (3 mm) long. Roll each piece into a small ball. Cover four of them with plastic wrap and set them aside.

3 Using the blunt end of the paintbrush, make two shallow depressions for the eye sockets in the circle of clay. Brush each depression lightly with water. Gently press two balls into place with your finger. Make an indentation in the center of each ball with the end of the brush.

4 Cut a ⅜-inch (9.5 mm) length from your coil and pinch each end to make the long, slender nose. Brush a line of water down the center of the face, position the coil, and lightly press it into place along the sides.

5 Roll out some clay to the thickness of three playing cards. Cut it into five shapes, as shown in figure 1. Brush the surface of the face with water, position the shapes, and lightly press them into place. With the craft knife, trim away the excess clay so it's flush with the edge of the circle. Cut a texture into the surface of the added layers. As the clay begins to dry, cut some more to enhance the texture.

Tools & Materials

.2 ounce (5.4 g) slow-fire lump silver metal clay

Syringe silver metal clay

Circle template, 1½ inch (3.8 mm) diameter

Pin tool

Toothbrush

Craft knife

Playing cards

Three-part sterling silver pin set [pin catch, joint, and 1-inch-long (2.5-cm) nickel pin stem]

Liver of sulfur

Polishing cloth

Burnisher

6 To make the bottom lip, pinch one of the remaining balls into a triangular shape. Brush the area below the nose with water and add it on. Roll a small, thin coil for the top lip. Attach it to the top of the bottom lip with water. Trim off any excess clay with the craft knife.

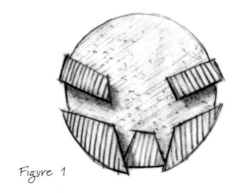

Figure 1

7 For the horns, roll out a thick coil, ¼ inch (6 mm) in diameter and at least 2 inches (5 cm) long. Cut it in half and taper one end of each.

8 With the rolling pin, slightly flatten each of the wider ends of the horns. Brush them with water, position them, and firmly press them into place. Place one of the balls at the base of each horn and the third in the center of the forehead. Lightly press them down, flattening each one slightly. Bend the horns toward each other.

9 Once the mask is bone dry, fire it at 1,650°F (900°C) for two hours. Let the piece cool. Attach the pin back, as described on pages 46–47.

10 Wire brush the surface, then apply a blue-gray liver of sulfur patina. Use a polishing cloth to polish the raised surfaces back to silver. Burnish the textured areas to create a high contrast to the background.

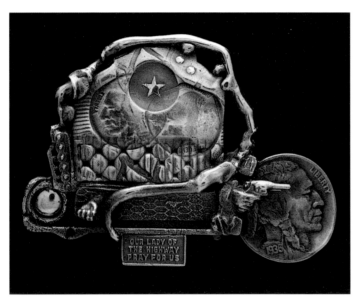

J. Fred Woell. *Road Kill,* 1997.
1 ¾ x 2½ x ⅜ in. (4.4 cm x 6.4 cm x 9.5 mm). Metal clay; cast sterling, nickel.
PHOTO BY ARTIST.

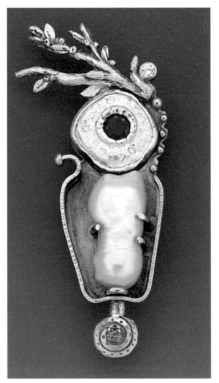

Nancy Karpel. *Wisdom Brooch,* 2001.
2½ x 1¹⁄₁₆ x ¼ in. (6.4 x 2.7 cm x 6 mm). Metal clay; CZ and garnet, 18k gold, 14k gold, freshwater pearl, tourmaline, sterling silver; oxidized.
PHOTO BY FRANK POOLE.

Tic Tac Toe Tie Tac

Capture your passion
for the classic
childhood game in
pure silver.

Instructions

1 Roll out metal clay to the thickness of three playing cards.

2 Use a craft knife and cut a square of clay that measures 1¼ x 1¼ inches (3.2 x 3.2 cm). Use the corner of a playing card as a template to round off the sharp corners.

3 Extrude a grid on the surface of the clay square. Start the grid lines off the edge of the square. Allow to dry to bone dry.

4 Use the craft knife to trim the excess grid lines. File the edges with the fine emery board.

5 Fashion a coil of clay with your fingers, then use the see-through ruler or plate glass to finish it to ⅛ inch (3 mm) in diameter and 5 inches (12.7 cm) long.

6 Brush water around the outside edge of the square and wrap the coil around it. Make sure it touches the side edge all the way around but without resting on top.

7 Cut the coil where the ends overlap. Use the blender tool to blend the seam.

8 Use the pin tool to scribe the placement of the X's and O's. Create the X and O design with the syringe. Practice on your work surface before you work on the piece itself. Put any rejects into your slip jar.

Tools & Materials

.2 ounce (5.6 g) medium-fire lump silver metal clay

Syringe silver metal clay

Playing cards

Craft knife

Fine emery board

See-through ruler or sheet of plate glass with finished edges

Size #0 blender tool

Pin tool

Tumbler with stainless steel shot

Two-part epoxy

Nickel tie-tac post

9 Fire the bone-dry piece flat on a kiln shelf for 10 minutes at 1,650°F (900°C).

10 Wire brush the piece and tumble it for 25 minutes.

11 Dry the piece. Use two-part epoxy to attach the tie-tac post.

Under the Elm

I designed this pin as a fond remembrance of a special day under the tree's branches.

Instructions

1 Use the two-part silicone mold material to make a mold from tree bark. (See pages 33–34 for more information on mold making.)

2 Use mat-board spacers to roll out half the metal clay to 1/16 inch (1.6 mm) thick. Use the cured mold as you would a rubber stamp on the clay. Tear the textured clay into three parts then rejoin the layers by slightly overlapping them. Brush water on each seam and lightly press them with your finger.

3 Roll out the rest of the metal clay to the thickness of three playing cards. Brush with water and place the three-part stacked piece on top of the moist clay. Press the seams lightly with your finger to attach them. Trim the stacked clay into a 2¼ x 1⅛-inch (5.7 x 2.8 cm) rectangle, with the tissue blade (see figure 1).

Figure 1

4 From the excess, make a marble-size ball. Let the ball sit unwrapped (don't moisten it) for 10 minutes. Use the rest of the clay to make a coil measuring ⅛ inch (3 mm) in diameter and 3 inches (7.6 cm) long. The coil should have cracks and imperfections on the surface, complementing the tree bark texture.

5 Brush a line of water onto the rectangle, then lay the coil on it. Brush both sides of the coil with water to ensure a good attachment. Press it lightly with your finger. Trim the coil to fit. Let the piece dry completely.

Tools & Materials

.4 ounce (11.2 g) slow-fire lump silver metal clay

Syringe medium-fire metal clay

Two-part silicone mold material

Piece of heavily textured bark

Playing cards

Tissue blade

Circle pattern cutter, ⅜ inch (9.5 mm) diameter

Plastic drinking straw

Cubic zirconia, ¼ inch (6 mm) diameter

Craft knife

Size #0 blender tool

Three-part pin set [sterling silver pin catch, joint, and 1½-inch-long (3.8 cm) nickel pin stem]

Liver of sulfur

Nylon scrubbing pad

6 Set the stone with the syringe lip stone setting; see page 39. Allow the clay to dry.

7 Cut out a ¼-inch (6 mm) section of the dry coil for the stone (see photo for position). Set the bezel in place. Extrude a line of syringe clay around the base of the bezel. Use the blender tool to remove any excess clay.

8 Fire the bone-dry pin, lying flat on a kiln shelf, at 1,650°F (900°C) for two hours. Allow the piece to air cool. Attach the pin catch and joint. Follow the directions on pages 46–47.

9 Wire brush the surface, then apply a patina with liver-of-sulfur patina to blue-gray. Scrub the silver with the nylon scrubbing pad. These scrubbing tools won't scratch the stone.

Honeycomb Button

*What could be
more enticing
than pure silver
buttons on a
special garment?*

Instructions for One Button

1 On top of the plastic texture sheet, roll out the metal clay to ¹⁄₁₆ inch (1.6 mm) thick.

2 Use the craft knife to cut a 1¼ inch (3.2-cm) square. Using the square template, cut a ½ inch (1.3-cm) opening in the center of the square. Round the corners as you cut, because cracks can develop in sharp corners during drying.

3 On top of the fiberglass window screen, roll out more metal clay to ¹⁄₁₆ inch (1.6 mm) thick. Cut out a ¾-inch (1.9-cm) square from the new texture. Allow both squares to dry to leather hard.

4 On the plain (back) side of the clay, brush water around the rim of the square opening. Do the same on the textured side of the smaller square. Place the front side of the small square over the opening on the back of the larger square and press the pieces together firmly.

5 Using the blender tool, press a pattern around the seam for texture, as shown in figure 1. This also helps assure a good attachment. Allow the piece to dry to bone dry.

Figure 1

6 To make the button shank, roll some fresh metal clay into a pea-size ball. Slightly flatten the ball and cut a hole in it with the beverage stirrer. When it's bone dry, slice the "dough-nut" in half with the tissue blade.

Tools & Materials

.5 ounce (14 g) slow-fire lump silver metal clay

Plastic texture sheet with honeycomb design

Craft knife

Square template sheet, ½ inch (1.3 cm) opening

Fiberglass screen mesh, for texture

Size #6 blender tool

Beverage stirrer

Tissue blade

Plastic pallet knife

Alumina hydrate

Copper wire

Liver of sulfur

Polishing cloth

7 Use the pallet knife to add some thick metal clay slip to the end of the button shank (read about making slip on pages 26–27). Attach the shank to the center of the button's back.

8 Dust a ⅛-inch (3 mm) layer of alumina hydrate onto the kiln shelf and place the buttons face down, in the powder. Fire them at 1,650°F (900°C) for two hours.

9 To achieve the finish shown, first create a wire-brush finish. Hook a piece of copper wire through the button loop and dip it in a liver-of-sulfur patina solution until it has a blue-black color. (You might instead select a finish that matches a particular garment.) Rub the button with a polishing cloth to remove the patina from the high areas, leaving dark color in low areas to accentuate the texture.

Silver Lace Button

Silver complements almost any fabric texture or color. Put these brilliant, lacy buttons on a jacket or blouse.

Instructions for One Button

Because the two clay formulas each have a different shrinkage rate, firing them together creates an interesting effect. The extruded syringe clay causes the button's original circle shape (which is made of high-shrinkage, slow-fire clay) to draw itself into a dome. Refer to figure 1 on page 55.

1 Use mat-board spacers to roll the slow-fire metal clay to 1/16 inch (1.6 mm) thick.

2 Use the pin tool to trace out the circle on the surface of the metal clay. Let the clay reach bone dry.

3 Sand the edges of the circle with the coarse emery board, then with the fine one.

4 Brush water on the bone-dry circle to make the surface damp. Extrude clay from the syringe, holding it 1/4 inch (6 mm) above the surface. You don't need to practice this technique; let it fall in a design that's pleasing to you. Store the tip of the syringe in the vial. Let the clay reach bone dry.

5 To make the button shank, slightly flatten a pea-size ball of slow-fire clay. Cut a hole in it with the stirrer. When the piece is bone dry, cut it in half with a tissue blade.

6 Use the pallet knife to add a little thick slip to the ends of a shank, and attach the shank to the center back of the button.

Tools & Materials

.1 ounce (5.6 g) slow-fire metal clay

Syringe medium- or quick-fire metal clay

Pin tool

A quarter or a circle template, 1 inch (2.5 cm) diameter

Coarse and fine emery boards

Cut-flower water vial, filled with water

Beverage stirrer

Tissue blade

Plastic pallet knife

Alumina hydrate

Tumbler with stainless steel shot

7 Dust a thin layer of alumina hydrate on a kiln shelf and place the button, face side down, in the powder. Fire the clay at 1,650°F (900°C) for 2 hours.

8 Wire brush with soap and water, then tumble the button in stainless steel shot for 20 minutes. The button itself retains its satin finish, contrasting nicely with the high polish of the "lace."

Dots & Doughnuts

Fabulous
hollow-form
designs, such as
this funky bead
covered in
circles and dots,
are easy to do
with metal clay.

Instructions for a Basic Hollow Bead with End Caps

1. Apply glue to a 1-inch (2.5 cm) polystyrene sphere on a bamboo skewer, as described on pages 32–33. Fabric glue remains slightly tacky, even when dry.

2. Use mat-board spacers to roll out the clay to ¹⁄₁₆ inch (1.6 mm).

3. Use the pin tool to cut out two 1-inch (2.5-cm) circles from the clay. These will cover the northern and southern hemispheres of your bead. Use the craft knife to cut out a strip of clay 3½ inches (8.9 cm) long and ½ inch (1.3 cm) wide. This will be the bead's equator.

4. Remove the glue-covered polystyrene ball from the skewer. Place the two circles on the top and bottom of the sphere. The metal clay will stick nicely to the tacky surface. Add the equator piece, as shown in figure 1, and brush the seams with a little water. Blend the seams with a blender tool until they disappear. Put the silver clay–covered bead back onto the skewer.

5. To make the end caps, roll out a marble-size piece of clay ¹⁄₁₆-inch (1.6 mm) thick. Cut two circles with the piece of brass tubing. Cut a hole in each center with a plastic drinking straw. Thread these onto each end of the bamboo skewer, one for each hole. Moisten the surface and press each end cap lightly into place.

Tools & Materials

.5 ounce (14 g) medium-fire lump silver metal clay

Polystyrene sphere, 1 inch (2.5 cm) diameter

Bamboo skewer

Round paintbrush

Fabric glue

Pin tool

A quarter or circle template, 1 inch (2.5 cm) diameter

Craft knife

Size #0 blender tool

Piece of brass tubing, ½ inch (1.3 cm) diameter

Plastic drinking straw

Terra-cotta saucer

Support material

Liver of sulfur

Burnisher

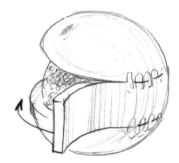

Figure 1

Instructions for the Decoration

1 Make three more doughnuts and use them to decorate the surface of the bead.

2 Roll out some clay to 1/16 inch (1.6 mm) thick. Cut 31 circles with the plastic drinking straw. Moisten the surface of the clay-covered bead and press the circles lightly into place (keep the circles tented under plastic wrap while you decorate so they don't dry out).

3 Fire the bone-dry piece in a terra-cotta saucer filled with support material. To prevent slumping, submerge the bead halfway into the support material. Fire outdoors or with good ventilation to avoid the polystyrene's toxic fumes in the initial firing stage.

4 Wire brush the piece. Apply a blue-black liver-of-sulfur patina. Use the burnishing tool to highlight the dots, doughnuts, and end caps.

Barbara Becker Simon. *Ant Bead*, 1998, 1⅞ x 1½ x 1½ in. (4.7 x 3.8 x 3.8 cm). Hollow formed silver metal clay bead with syringe application. PHOTO BY ROB STEGMANN.

Barbara Becker Simon. *Study in Grey and White II*, 2000. 23½ x 1⅛ x 1⅛ in. (59.7 x 2.8 x 2.8 cm). Silver metal clay hollow beads and hollow lamp-worked beads by the artist. PHOTO BY LARRY SANDERS.

Stormy Wave

This slip texture suggests a view from high above the earth. Dramatically highlight the bead's surface by creating a strong contrast to its dark patina with a high-polish, hand-burnished finish.

Tools & Materials

.5 ounce (14 g) medium-fire lump silver
  metal clay

Polystyrene sphere, 1 inch (2.5 cm) diameter

Bamboo skewer

Round paintbrush

Fabric glue

Pin tool

A quarter or a circle template, 1 inch
  (2.5 cm) diameter

Craft knife

Size #0 blender tool

Brass tubing, ½ inch (1.3 cm) diameter

Plastic drinking straw

Plastic pallet knife

Terra-cotta saucer

Support material

Liver of sulfur

Burnisher

Instructions

To make a hollow bead you need to start with a core material that will burn away. See pages 32–33 for more information on core materials.

1 Make a Basic Hollow Sphere with End Caps, as described in steps 1–5 on page 127.

2 Use the plastic pallet knife to add thick slip to the surface of the bead. (Directions for making slip are on pages 26–27.) Try to get as many peaks as possible for dramatic texture. See page 31 for more about slip texture.

3 Let the bead dry to bone dry and fire it in a terra-cotta saucer filled with support material. Submerge it halfway into the support material or the walls could slump during the fire. Fire outside, or with good ventilation, because polystyrene emits toxic fumes during firing.

4 Wire brush the bead. Apply a blue-black patina with liver of sulfur, then burnish the bead by hand, highlighting the peaks and the end caps.

Lotus Leaves

The curving, leafy shapes that embrace this charming hollow bead give it an appliqué effect. Its carved leaf-veins enhance the impression of flowing, organic movement.

Tools & Materials

.5 ounce (14 g) slow-fire lump silver
   metal clay

Polystyrene sphere, 1 inch (2.5 cm)
   diameter

Bamboo skewer

Watercolor paintbrush

Fabric glue

Pin tool

A quarter or a circle template, 1 inch
   (2.5 cm) diameter

Craft knife

Size #0 blender tool

Piece of brass tubing, ½ inch (1.3 cm)
   diameter

Plastic drinking straw

Linoleum carving tool

Terra-cotta saucer

Support material

Liver of sulfur

Tumbler with stainless steel shot

Instructions

1 Make a Basic Hollow Sphere with End Caps, as described in steps 1–5 on page 127.

2 Use the craft knife to cut four or more leaf shapes of various sizes. Moisten the surface and lightly press them into place. Let the bead dry to bone dry.

3 Use the linoleum carving tool to cut veins down the centers of the leaves. Review the instructions for the carving technique on pages 35–36. Keep in mind that carving on a curved surface is more challenging than carving on a flat plane.

4 Carve the edges of the leaves with the craft knife so they taper into the bead's surface.

5 Mix some very thin slip to the consistency of milk. With a small watercolor brush, paint the slip onto the background of the bead. Let it dry and add another layer of slip. Repeat this as many times as you like to build a subtle background texture to make a nice contrast to the leaf shapes. See page 30 for more about thinned-paste texture.

6 Let the last slip layer dry then fire the bead in a terra cotta saucer filled with support material. Submerge the bead halfway into the support material or the walls could slump during firing. Remember to vent the kiln, or fire it outdoors, as described in the section on burnout materials on page 41.

7 Wire brush the bead. Apply a blue-gray patina with liver of sulfur. Tumble the piece in stainless steel shot for 25 minutes to create the mirror finish on the raised portions of the design.

Avocado Salt Cellar

Feeling adventuresome? Use the natural textures of various kinds of fruit to make a series of little bowls to dress up the dinner table or give away as hostess gifts. The brilliant enamel liner is an eye-catcher.

Instructions

1. Use the two-part silicone mold material to make a mold from the bottom half of an avocado. (See pages 33–34 for more information on mold making.) Allow the mold to cure. Remove the avocado and throw it away.

2. Press the entire package of metal clay into the mold with your thumb. (If you've ever made a pinch pot, this is a similar technique.) Allow the metal clay to dry in the mold overnight. Remove the metal clay from the mold and continue to dry it to bone dry.

3. Set the metal clay bowl in a terra-cotta saucer filled with support material. Fire the piece at 1,650°F (900°C) for 10 minutes. Although this formula of metal clay sinters in one minute, the longer firing time will create a denser material that is better suited for enameling. Let it cool to room temperature before removing it from the kiln.

4. While the bowl is cooling, wash the enamel. Transparent enamel must first be washed free of its smaller particles so it won't be cloudy. Fill the film container one-fourth of the way full with the transparent enamel. Add tap water and stir the solution vigorously with the rod. Count to ten, then pour out the cloudy water. Only the large grains of enamel should be left at the bottom. Repeat this step several times, until the water remains clear after a count of ten. Pour off this water and do a final wash with distilled water to remove any of the minerals from the tap water. Pour the wet enamel into the dish. Leave it in a clean and dust-free area to dry. When the enamel is dry, place it in the 60-mesh enamel sifter.

5. To prepare the inside of the bowl for enameling, scrub it with the pumice powder. Rinse the bowl well to remove all the pumice, dry it, then brush the inside of the bowl with clear-fire solution diluted with an equal amount of distilled water.

6. Dust the inside of the bowl evenly with a ⅛-inch (3 mm) layer of enamel from the sifter. Allow the enamel to dry completely.

7. Preheat the kiln to 1,500°F (800°C). Place the bowl on the kiln shelf and put the shelf in the kiln for 3 minutes. This amount of time is a general guide, because each enamel color has its own fusing point. When the inside of the bowl is clear and glassy, remove it from the kiln and let it cool. If you like the results, the enameling is finished, but it can be repeated. Brush the inside of the bowl with the clear-fire solution, then sift another layer of powdered enamel onto it. Let it dry, and fire again.

8. Wire brush the exterior metal area, then tumble the piece for 20 minutes.

Tools & Materials

1 ounce (28 g) quick-fire lump silver metal clay

Two-part silicone mold material

Avocado

Terra-cotta saucer

Support material

Transparent enamel

See-through film container

Glass or clear plastic rod

Distilled water

Glass or ceramic dish

60-mesh enamel sifter

Pumice powder

Clear-fire solution (available where jewelers' enameling supplies are sold)

Tumbler with stainless steel shot

Fancy Filigreed Box

I covered this little trinket with delicate tracery reminiscent of one of my favorite styles of ornamentation.

Instructions

Making little boxes from metal clay is one of my favorite ways to use this great medium. It's similar to the traditional metalsmithing technique, but much faster. I make a model using index cards to help me work out the proportions and make better design decisions. Once the design is built, I cut it apart and trace the pattern pieces in the clay.

Tools & Materials

1.1 ounces (30.8 g) medium-fire silver metal clay
Medium-fire syringe metal clay
Index cards
Rubber stamp, filligreed heart design
Craft knife
Clear gel-type water-soluble glue
Size #0 blender tool
Coarse and fine emery boards
Alumina hydrate
Liver of sulfur
Burnisher

1. Cut these pieces from an index card:
   - 2 rectangles, 1 x 1⅜ inches (2.5 x 3.5 cm), for the lid and bottom
   - 2 rectangles, ¼ x 1¼ inches (6 mm x 3.2 cm), for the bottom's long sides
   - 2 rectangles, ¼ x ⅞ inch (6 mm x 2.2 cm), for the bottom's short sides
   - 2 rectangles, ¼ x 1 inch (6 mm x 2.5 cm), for the lid's long sides
   - 2 rectangles, ¼ by ¾ inch (6 mm x 1.9 cm), for the lid's short sides

2. Use mat-board spacers to roll out 1 ounce (28 g) of the lump clay to ¹⁄₁₆ inch (1.6 mm) thick. Use the rubber stamp to create an overall texture on the clay.

3. Cut out the pattern pieces for the box with the craft knife. Allow the pieces to dry to bone dry. When all the parts are dry and easy to handle, you're ready to assemble the box.

4. Glue together long and short bottom pieces into two separate "L" shapes. Allow the glue to dry for three to five minutes. Repeat for the long and short pieces for the lid. You should have four "L" shapes when you're finished.

5. Glue together the bottom two "L's." Repeat for the lid. Allow the glue to dry as before. The larger rectangle will be the walls of the box and the smaller one, the inside walls of the lid.

6. Carefully pick up the smaller rectangle and glue it to the inside lid of the box. Repeat for the bottom walls. Allow the glue to dry.

7. Use the metal clay syringe to run a line of metal clay down all the seams on the inside of the box. Wait for the wet clay to stiffen, then use the blender tool to push it into the seams.

8. Brush water onto the outside seams. Let the box bottom and box lid become bone dry. Test the fit of the lid. If it needs adjustment, use the emery board to file the edges or use the craft knife to carve away extra material.

9. Sprinkle a ⅛-inch (3 mm) layer of alumina hydrate on a kiln shelf and place the flat sides of the box onto it. The alumina will make the pieces shrink at the same rate, so they'll still fit together after they're fired. Fire the pieces at 1,650°F (900°C) for 10 minutes.

10. Wire brush the box. Dip the pieces in liver of sulfur to a red-violet and blue-purple patina. Hand burnish the edges to a mirror finish.

Twig & Leaf Condiment Spoon

Make a replica of any organic object, perfect in every detail. This makes an elegant hostess or wedding gift.

Instructions

This project isn't as difficult as it is time-consuming. I suggest you work on other projects in between, allowing the layers to dry while you enjoy a perfectly productive afternoon.

1 Select a twig with a natural V-shape fork in it (I used an elm twig from my backyard). Make it any length you like, as long as it will still fit into your kiln.

2 Use the empty syringe to measure 1 cc of distilled water into a new jar of metal clay paste. Mix it well with the wooden craft stick, being careful not to create bubbles as you stir. Allow the mixture to sit for 10 minutes, then stir it again. This allows the water to be thoroughly absorbed by the binder.

3 Give the mixture a good stir, then use the watercolor brush to paint a thin layer of diluted paste directly on the twig. Allow the paste to dry thoroughly. Repeat, until you have applied 10 to 12 layers. Remember to stir the paste before you add the next layer because the silver particles quickly settle to the bottom.

4 When the last layer is dry, support the twig in a bed of vermiculite and fire it at 1,650°F (900°C) for 20 minutes.

5 After firing you'll probably find cracks in the metal clay as a result of unevenly applied layers. Fill cracks with paste and allow it to dry. To hide the repair, paint a new layer of slip over it. Once it's dry, fire it again (supported in the vermiculite) at 1,650°F (900°C) for 10 minutes.

Tools & Materials

1.1 ounces (30.8 g) silver metal clay paste
.1 ounce (2.8 g) medium-fire metal clay
Twig with a natural "V" shape
Empty syringe
Distilled water
Wooden craft stick
Watercolor paintbrush
Vermiculite
Skeleton leaf (available at craft supply stores)
Craft knife
Size #0 blender tool
Cotton swab
Liver of sulfur

6 Use mat-board spacers to roll out a ¹⁄₁₆ inch (1.6 mm) layer of clay. Lay the skeleton leaf on the surface, pressing down lightly so the leaf sticks to the clay. Roll the rolling pin across the top of the leaf to be sure you capture all the intricate details in the veins.

7 Use the craft knife to cut out the shape of the leaf.

8 Allow the leaf and clay to dry together, then fire them, lying flat on a kiln shelf, at 1,650°F (900°C) for 10 minutes. The leaf will burn away, leaving its incredible detail behind.

9 Lay ⅛-inch-thick (3mm) coil along the edge of the leaf, then press the leaf onto the twig (see figure 1). For added support, I attached another coil along the center of the back. Make a tapered coil, ¼ inch (6mm) thick at its wider end, that is equal to three-quarters of the length of the leaf. Brush water on the coil and use the blender tool to create a smooth connection.

10 Allow the added coils of clay to dry to bone dry, then support the construction in a bed of vermiculite and fire it for 10 minutes at 1,650°F (900°C).

11 To finish the piece, scrub it with a wire brush and soap and water. To obtain a range of magenta, red-violet, and blue-purple colors on the leaf, apply a weak solution of liver of sulfur with a cotton swab. The color will build slowly; when you reach the colors you like, stop the chemical reaction by rinsing it under cold running water for 1 minute. If you plan to use the piece for food, don't use a patina.

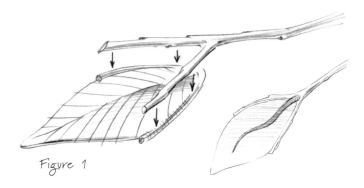

Figure 1

Eleanor Moty. *Earrings*, 1996.
1 ¼ x 1 x ⅛ in. (3.1 cm x 2.5 cm x 3 mm). 24k metal clay; fabricated with sterling silver, 22k gold, and tanzanite.
PHOTO BY ARTIST.

Perfume Amphora

In the golden age of Greece, people used amphorae to transport wine and olive oil by ship to exotic destinations all around the Mediterranean. Fill this graceful vessel shape with your favorite fragrance.

Instructions

This amphora is constructed from six different parts: the body, neck, lip, stopper, and two handles. The pieces are assembled when the clay is bone dry, using metal clay slip.

1 To make this hollow vessel form you'll need to build a core made of several different layers. Use the craft knife to cut a 1 x 1 x 2-inch (2.5 x 2.5 x 5 cm) rectangle from a piece of green floral foam. Carve the floral foam into the teardrop shape of the vessel's body. Use your fingers to push into the foam, refining the shape.

2 With the skewer, pierce the floral foam at the top center of the body of the vessel where the neck will be.

3 Paint a thick layer of fabric glue on the surface of the floral foam. Allow it to dry overnight. (Wash out the brush as soon as you're finished or the glue will ruin it.)

4 Paint a second layer of glue, thinner than the first, on the surface, and allow it to dry. The fabric glue will remain slightly tacky, even when dry.

5 The third layer of the core is made from a special formula of paper clay that won't burn away during the firing. Roll out a walnut-size piece of paper clay to $\frac{1}{16}$ inch (1.6 mm) thick.

6 Using figure 1 as a template (photocopied at 160%), cut out the pieces with the pin tool. Cut a hole in the center of the circle with the straw.

Tools & Materials

1.1 ounces (30.8 g) medium-fire lump silver metal clay

Green floral foam

Craft knife

Bamboo skewer

Round paintbrush

Fabric glue

1 ounce (28g) paper clay made of paper pulp, volcanic ash, and talc

Pin tool

Plastic beverage straw

Size #0 blender tool

Craft stick

Circle pattern cutter, ½ inch (1.3 cm) diameter

Sheet of plate glass with finished edges

Terra-cotta saucer

Support material

Liver of sulfur

Hot glue gun and glue stick

Faceted peridot bead strand, 18 inches (45.7 cm) long

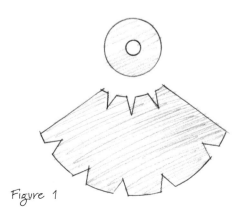

Figure 1

7 Remove the skewer from the glue-covered floral foam. Center the circle on the top of the core, then add the body piece (see figure 2). The paper clay will stick nicely to the tacky surface of the fabric glue. Re-skewer the piece and brush the paper clay seams with a little water. Use the blender tool to bring the seams together.

Figure 2

8 Allow the paper clay to dry completely. If metal clay is laid over still-moist paper clay, trapped water may cause the vessel to rupture during firing. Apply another layer of glue.

9 Roll out the metal clay to ¹⁄₁₆ inch (1.6 mm) thick, and cover the core with it, following steps 6 and 7.

10 Re-roll the leftover scraps of clay to ¹⁄₁₆ inch (1.6 mm) thick. For the amphora's neck, cut a strip ³⁄₈ inches (9.5 mm) wide and 1 inch (2.5 cm) long. Wrap the band around the end of a pencil and use the blender tool to close the seam.

11 Make a coil from a pea-size ball of metal clay. Cut the coil in half. Moisten the seam of the neck, then lay a piece of the coil over it. Position the other coil on the opposite side. Use the end of the blender tool to press a textured pattern into the coils (see figure 3). Let the neck dry to bone dry.

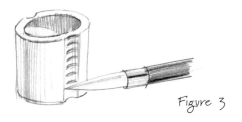

Figure 3

12 Roll out some leftover scraps of clay to the thickness of a craft stick. Cut a circle ½ inch (1.3 cm) in diameter. Cut the center of the circle with the straw, and dry it to bone dry.

13 Use the plate glass to roll out a ⅛ x 2-inch (3 mm x 5.1 cm) coil. Cut two pieces, each ⅞ inch (2.2 cm) long. Shape these into a pair of "C" shapes; allow them to become bone dry. Use the craft knife to cut these handles to fit to the body, just below the neck.

14 Attach all the parts together with thick slip and blend the seams. Set the amphora aside to dry to bone dry.

15 To make the stopper, roll a ball of clay to ¼ inch (6 mm) in diameter. Place this on the work surface and roll a taper on one end to make an elongated egg shape. Place it on the top of the amphora to check the fit. Let bone it dry.

16 Lay the stopper and the amphora vessel horizontally and not touching, in a terra-cotta saucer filled with support material, at 1,650°F (900°C) for 20 minutes. Even though medium-fire metal clay fires in 10 minutes, the longer time makes sure the floral foam completely burns away.

17 Wire brush the silver. Dip it in a weak solution of liver-of-sulfur patina until you've built up a warm gold color with a hint of rose.

18 Dip the end of the stopper in a puddle of hot glue. This creates a seal for the stopper. Thread the strand of faceted peridot beads through the amphora's handles.

GLOSSARY OF TERMS

Bail a loop or piece of metal used to hang a pendant on a necklace

Bezel the thin strip of metal used to hold a decorative stone

Bone dry all the water in the clay has evaporated; only the binder and silver particles remain

Burnish to compress the surface of fired metal with a metal tool

Crash cool after firing, rapid cooling of dichroic glass within the kiln to 1000°F (538°C), then cooling kiln to room temperature; prevents devitrification

Devitrification clouding of dichroic glass

Extrude to force a small coil of clay through the tip of a syringe-type container

Fine silver pure silver, marked "999" or "FS"

Fuse join metal to metal without the use of solder

Hallmark a mark stamped or scribed on a piece of jewelry that indicates the type of metal used

Inclusion any nonmetal, permanent element in the design that will be fired with the clay

Kiln high-temperature oven

Leather hard clay that is firm and somewhat flexible, like leather; most but not all of the moisture is gone

Oxidize tarnishing or darkening of metal

Patina color obtained by chemical treatment of metal; oxidation or antique finish

Quench to quickly cool hot metal by dipping it into a water bath

Rehydrate to recondition dried clay by adding water

Slip clay mixed with a high proportion of water

Sinter when metal clay particles fuse or bond together; silver sinters at 1,650°F (900°C); gold at 1,830°F (1000°C)

Slump collapsing or warping of a form during firing due to the forces of heat and gravity

Step down reducing the firing temperature of the metal clay while extending its firing time

Sterling silver an alloy of 95 percent fine silver and 5 percent copper

CONTRIBUTING ARTISTS

Susan Amendolara, Edinboro, Pennsylvania
Page 91

Robert Dancik, South Salem, New York
Page 7

Chris Darway, Lambertville, New Jersey
Page 15, 97

Mary Ann Devos, Fort Myers Beach, Florida
Page 44

Debra Dressler, Lakeland, Minnesota
Page 24

Celie Fago, Bethel, Vermont
Page 102

Dawn Hale, Hampton, New Jersey
Page 41

Hadar Jacobson, Berkeley, California
Page 47

Nancy Karpel, New Haven, Connecticut
Page 102, 117

Linda Kaye-Moses, Pittsfield, Massachusetts
Page 7, 37

Terry Kovalcik, Haledon, New Jersey
Page 35

Judy Kuskin, Seattle, Washington
Page 23

Tim McCreight, Portland, Maine
Page 25

Eleanor Moty, Tucson, Arizona
Page 139

Suz O'Dell, San Francisco, California
Page 27

Barbara Becker Simon, Cape Coral, Florida
Page 39, 40, 94, 128

Carl Stanley, Santa Barbara, California
Page 85

Candice Wakumoto, Mililani, Hawaii
Page 88

J. Fred Woell, Deer Isle, Maine
Page 117

A BIG THANK YOU TO

Kevin Whitmore, my fairy godfather, for recommending my name to Carol Taylor of Lark Books. It was his name I cursed at every deadline, but it is to him I owe the unending gratitude of having the opportunity to write this book;

Tim McCreight, for giving me both technical and emotional support. Thanks for being my coach and cheerleader. I once called you mentor and now I call you friend;

the five most talented artists with whom I have the privilege to work: **Barbara Becker Simon, Carl Stanley, Celie Fago, Chris Darway,** and **J. Fred Woell.** I am grateful for the generous time and technical knowledge you shared with me and which contributed depth and variety to these pages;

all the immensely talented artists who contributed work to the gallery section of the book. I wish we could have included each and every image. I am proud to show your work, which is sure to inspire metal clay artists for years to come;

Akira Nishio, Juichi Hirasawa, and **Darnall Burks**, of Mitsubishi Materials Corporation, who have been generous with technical information and resources;

my editor, **Suzanne Tourtillott**, who I saw as my guide throughout this journey; art director **Celia Naranjo**, for the creative vision that makes me look good; and photographer **Sandy Stanbaugh**, for her excellent work and for providing enjoyable evenings after our work day was over;

Rob Pulleyn, Lark Books' publisher, and **Carol Taylor**, publishing director, for providing me with the opportunity to write this book. Thank you for waiting;

Maddy Weisz, Phil Hendricks, Pete Wire, Jean Jones, Jo and Randy Luttrell, Nancy and Mark O'Donnell, Craig, Cyndy, Mayah, and **Will DeMartino** for understanding when I couldn't come out to play;

my very cool parents, **Dan and Debby Wire.** Their love and support has allowed me to have the confidence and courage to attempt anything I have ever wanted to do; and

George Parrish, my husband, who still remains my friend and copilot through this life. I appreciate all your hours of pre-proofreading; I couldn't fathom tackling this project without your love and encouragement.

INDEX